A While Longer

Greg J. Cring

The decree of the Congregation for the Propagation of the Faith, A.A.S., 58, 1186 (approved by Pope Paul VI on 14 October 1966) states that the *Nihil Obstat* and *Imprimatur* are no longer required on publications that deal with private revelations, provided they contain nothing contrary to faith and morals. The author wishes to manifest his unconditional submission to the final and official judgment of the magisterium of the Church regarding the events at Garabandal and those presently under investigation at Medjugorje.

Cover design by Greg J. Cring
Cover Illustrations: Front: Greg J. Cring: Third Secret of Fatima Vision
Back: Photo from www.medjugorje.ws, used with permission, and Greg J. Cring: Climbing Cross Mountain at Medjugorje
Interior design and images by Greg J. Cring

ISBN: 1463562543
ISBN-13: 978-1463562540

Dedication

In thanks to God,
for my family, especially my wife Suey, my children Heidi and Patrick, my
mother Mary, and my father Harold, and for my spiritual mother, the
Blessed Virgin Mary.

Table of Contents

Introduction

I didn't know what the word "faith" meant.

My father had both a keen intellect and the gift of common sense so he could break life's events down to their essence. He could quickly determine "that is good" or "that is bad". Fortunately, he handed down some of this to his children.

But the most important gift he imparted to his children was the gift of faith. I was unaware I had been given this gift until I needed it. While never doubting in God or His love for us, in time I met many who did. In college and the workforce I spent many a Friday Happy Hour arguing points of faith over pitchers of beer and beer nuts. The memory of not being able to convince those without faith still lingers. As I said, I did not yet really understand what the word "faith" meant.

My Grandmother on my mother's side had more faith than an entire church of worshippers. She lived with us for many years after her husband died, which happened when I was young. Occasionally I would find letters she absentmindedly left on the end table, full multi-page letters to Jesus. She was always smiling and content. It was only later that I learned she had a very bad childhood. Grandma was an orphan who had been raised by a malicious woman in a real Cinderella story. The woman had treated Grandma harshly, but after years of searching her brother finally found her and brought her back to Philadelphia where she lived with kind and sympathetic relatives. On learning of Grandma's childhood I felt sick. I wanted so badly to get even with that very uncaring woman. Of course, the woman had died many years earlier so it was simply a teenager's passion bubbling up — I did not have the means to pursue it. It was then that I remembered her letters to Jesus, and I wondered how the Master of the Universe who is Love itself allowed my sweet Grandma to suffer so much as a child. It was then that I began to learn the meaning of the word "faith".

Born in 1903, Grandma had lived through the sinking of the Titanic and told us stories about it. She told us the company owners of the Titanic had the words "Not Even God Can Sink This Ship" placed on the ship's bottom. Of course, she said, it sank on its first voyage and many died because of the owners' pride. Grandma could never talk about the Great Depression without crying, even fifty years later. With tears welling up in her eyes she would remember the endless lines of unemployed men and soldiers waiting for a bowl of soup, and walking past broken men selling apples on street corners trying to get money to buy necessities for their children.

It was Grandmother who first told me about the apparitions of Blessed Mary at Fatima in 1917. Naively believing everyone felt like I did, I wished so much that I had been alive to be present at the apparition. Then in 1985 I heard about an ongoing apparition at a place called Medjugorje. I thought now I would have my chance to attend an apparition, as long as it kept happening! I remembered the Fatima visions had lasted for six months and so I thought these too would end soon and I would not have the opportunity to go there. Once I found out where they were happening, several thoughts occurred to me. Why there, in the middle of nowhere? Then I remembered that Fatima had been nowhere too until the apparitions. Why now? That I could not answer. How long will it last? It turns out it has continued now for thirty years, and it is continuing even at this writing!

I finally got my chance to attend an apparition without travelling to Medjugorje. Seer Ivan Dragicevic came to Austin, Texas and in the St. Louis King of France Catholic Church experienced an apparition of Blessed Mary while everyone prayed the Rosary. The church was crammed. Outside, the throng encircled the building, the people standing or being fortunate enough to sit in the folding chairs set up around the church. Speakers were wired to broadcast the event to those outside.

Fortunately I arrived early enough to get a balcony seat from where I could see everything. It was humid and confined, and we were packed in tight. Numerous priests in their finest vestments lined the altar. Even with the usual coughing and children crying over the Rosary prayers, the charged atmosphere remained. The tension from our expectations stifled us more than the humidity.

Ivan knelt and everyone stopped and stared while he had his apparition of Our Lady right in front of us! It was as if the entire gathering held its collected breath. My childhood dream to be present at an apparition of Our Lady was happening! After a few minutes, it was over. Then Ivan spoke to the crowd and took questions, helped by a translator. As the minutes passed, awareness grew within me. A few moments earlier Our Lady had actually come down from heaven to be present with us and had spoken to one of us. Yet everything before and after the apparition remained the same. It was then that I fully understood the meaning of the word "faith". I finally understood that God is really and truly present at every moment and that it is up to us to believe it. It is up to us to believe all that He told us in His Gospels. It is up to us to believe without seeing and to live His words of truth every day. Unlike a Hollywood movie, no special music cues up to signal that God is now present on screen.

My Grandmother instilled in me a fascination about Our Lady and Fatima which has remained with me to this day. I have read many books on both Fatima and the apparitions of Medjugorje. My interest has progressed from one of amazement to curiosity and finally to a desire to understand why they have occurred. From studying them, I have learned that while there have been many reported apparitions of Blessed Mary throughout the past two thousand years, none have been like those at the approved Fatima site and the yet unapproved Medjugorje site. Never doubting the truth of her apparitions, I realize God provides these particular apparitions of the twentieth century for a profound purpose. Using Scripture, messages from private revelations, my own insights, and my own faith in a merciful God, with humility I hope to explain the fruits of my research.

God bless you.

I will take Francisco and Jacinta [to Heaven] soon, but you must remain a while longer. Jesus wishes to use you to make me better known and loved.
Our Lady of Fatima to Lucia, 13 June 1917

PART I

The Church Age

The Age of the Church is that period of time from the days of the Apostles until the present. Before Jesus ascended to His Father, He gave the disciples the Great Commission, commanding them to go and teach all nations His Gospel message, and to baptize everyone in the name of the Father, and the Son, and the Holy Spirit. Spanning two thousand years, in this period the message of Jesus is preached throughout the world, and Catholic churches are established in all nations. The following chapters provide a synopsis of the Age of the Church.

Chapter 1
The Promise of His Coming

We see the first and second Comings of Jesus as two distinct events but it is actually one event in two parts, which mirrors the traditional Jewish wedding. In the first part of the Jewish wedding, erusin, the bride and groom are betrothed. At nisuin, the second part of the marriage ceremony, the wedding feast and consummation take place, and in ancient times this could happen a year after erusin. Between erusin and nisuin, the bride and groom remained in their respective homes, preparing for the second part of the wedding. Considered fully and legally married although living apart, the couple could separate only with a bill of divorce. It was one marriage fulfilled in two parts. Even today the traditional Jewish wedding retains the two distinct parts, although they happen on the same day.

The Jewish wedding mirrors the marriage between God and His people. Most of the laws and customs about the wedding ceremony, its preparations and the wedding banquet date back to the Jewish Patriarchs and the giving of the Torah at Sinai. Sometimes the Chassidic wedding invitation reminds the guests of the wedding's significance:

> In the merit of bringing joy and happiness to the bride and groom, may we see the reaffirmation of the bond between God Almighty (the

groom) and the Jewish people (the bride) with the coming of the righteous Messiah imminently in our days.[1]

Jesus often used marriage metaphors when speaking about His kingdom, and He identified Himself as the bridegroom:

...some people came to him and said to him, 'Why is it that John's disciples and the disciples of the Pharisees fast, but your disciples do not?' Jesus replied, 'Surely the bridegroom's attendants cannot fast while the bridegroom is still with them? As long as they have the bridegroom with them, they cannot fast. But the time will come when the bridegroom is taken away from them, and then, on that day, they will fast.[2]

Between erusin and nisuin, the groom returned to his father's house and prepared a place for his bride. The preparation lasted about a year, and after all was ready he returned. Following this custom, Jesus told His disciples He would return for His bride, the people of God:

In my Father's house there are many dwelling places. If there were not, would I have told you that I am going to prepare a place for you? And if I go and prepare a place for you, I will come back again and take you to myself, so that where I am you also may be.[3]

In the ancient Jewish wedding ritual, wine played a prominent role, and in the modern Jewish wedding wine is still used in the blessings given at erusin and nisuin.

In the ancient form the bridegroom and his father would meet with the bride's family and present a ketubah, or wedding contract, to the intended bride and her father. The young man would pour a cup of wine, and if the bride-to-be accepted the proposal she drank from the cup. In the current form of the wedding the erusin or engagement rite is a simple ceremony marked by two blessings given by the presiding rabbi while holding a cup of wine. The first blessing over the wine is said at almost all joyous occasions:

---

[1] "The Jewish Wedding Guide", August 3, 2010. <www.jewish-history.com/minhag.htm>
[2] Catholic Online, Mark 2,18-20, June 14, 2010. <www.catholic.org/bible/book.php?id=53>
[3] USCCB-NAB-John 14:2-3, June 14, 2010. </www.usccb.org/nab/bible/mark/mark2.htm>.

Blessed are You, Lord our God, Master of the Universe, Who creates the fruit of the vine.

The second blessing is specific for the wedding ceremony:

Blessed are You, Lord our God, Master of the universe, Who has made us holy through His Commandments, and commanded us regarding illicit relations, and has forbidden to us the betrothed, and has permitted to us those whom we have married through Chupah and Kiddushin; Blessed are You, Lord our God, Who makes His people Israel holy through Chupah and Kiddushin.

After completing the second blessing the rabbi gives the cup of wine to the groom, who drinks from it. The cup is presented to the bride, who drinks from it, symbolizing her commitment to share her life with the groom and his family from that moment.

As priest and Rabbi at the Last Supper, Jesus performed the erusin ceremony with Himself as the groom and the disciples, the seeds of His Church, as the bride:

Then he took a cup [of wine], gave thanks, and gave it to them, and they all drank from it.[4]

At every Catholic Mass, this ritual is re-presented to remind us that the Church is the bride of Christ and that we have committed ourselves to remain faithful to the teachings of Jesus our Groom, teachings which come from His Father. The priest, in the person of the Groom, takes the cup and drinks from it. Then the cup is presented to the bride in turn and when we drink from it we proclaim our union with the family of God. Catholics believe the bread and wine are the body and blood of Jesus, making it a complete communion of bride and groom.

At Sinai, Moses sprinkled the sacrificial blood of the Old Covenant on the altar and the people of God. At the altar at each Mass, the people of God receive the sacrificial offering of the body and blood of the New (renewed) Covenant, the perfect sacrifice of Jesus.

Nisuin takes place with seven blessings over a cup of wine. Various Rabbis and relatives give these blessings; the one who offers the blessing is the first to drink from the cup, followed by the groom and then his bride.

---

[4] USCCB-NAB-Mark 14:23, June 14, 2010. <www.usccb.org/nab/bible/mark/mark14.htm>

Nisuin between the Messiah and His people is still to come. Jesus has not returned from His Father's house to claim His bride, and Jesus said as much at the Last Supper:

> *Amen, I say to you, I shall not drink again the fruit of the vine until the day when I drink it new in the kingdom of God.*[5]

In other words, He will drink it again when the kingdom of God is completely fulfilled upon His return. We are in the period between the two parts of the wedding. We are the bride awaiting the groom's return to consummate the wedding at nisuin.

The wedding began with the betrothal at the first coming of Jesus, which established the kingdom of God on earth: *Repent, for the kingdom of heaven is at hand.*[6]

The *Catechism of the Catholic Church* clarifies the Kingdom of God is already present:

> The kingdom of Christ [is] already present in mystery, on earth; the seed and the beginning of the kingdom.

> We are already at "the last hour." Already the final age of the world is with us, and the renewal of the world is irrevocably under way... Christ's kingdom already manifests its presence through the miraculous signs that attend its proclamation by the Church ... until all things are subjected to him.[7]

The kingdom of heaven will be handed over to the Father at His second coming:

> Then comes the end, when he hands over the kingdom to his God and Father, when he has destroyed every sovereignty and every authority and power.[8]

At the second coming, the kingdom exists because Jesus established it.

---

[5] USCCB-NAB-Mark 14:25, June 14, 2010. <www.usccb.org/nab/bible/mark/mark14.htm>
[6] USCCB-NAB-Matthew 3:2
[7] *Catechism of the Catholic Church* (Liguori, Mo: Liguori Publications, 1994) 669-670.
[8] USCCB-NAB-1 Corinthians 15:24

Jesus is with the Father and from there He will return to claim His bride. Meanwhile, His disciples are preparing the bride by preaching the Gospel to all peoples, thus preparing the kingdom of heaven here on earth, as explained in the following parable:

> *The kingdom of heaven may be likened to a king who gave a wedding feast for his son... The servants went out into the streets and gathered all they found, bad and good alike, and the hall was filled with guests. But when the king came in to meet the guests he saw a man there not dressed in a wedding garment. He said to him, 'My friend, how is it that you came in here without a wedding garment?' But he was reduced to silence. Then the king said to his attendants, 'Bind his hands and feet, and cast him into the darkness outside, where there will be wailing and grinding of teeth.'* [9]

The parable's key conflict is between the king and the man without a wedding garment. Jesus is using a wedding custom of the first-century Jewish people to explain the kingdom of heaven to His disciples. Guests at a wedding received a robe, and this robe made every guest equal regardless of social status or kinship to the newlyweds. All were honored and welcomed. The robe transformed each person into a member of the wedding event. In the early baptism ritual of the Church, a person shed his garments and walked into a pool of water and was baptized. Afterwards he received a clean white linen robe as a sign of his transformation into a member of the kingdom of heaven. Members of the kingdom are to act like it. In the parable, the man not wearing the robe wants to enjoy the feast with everyone else, but without being changed. He wants to keep to his old ways, and in the end he is cast out of the wedding banquet.

The first part of our wedding is finished and the plans for the second part are finalized, except for one detail. The guest list is not complete. Each time someone listens to a disciple of Jesus and accepts His teachings and is baptized, that person dons the white garment and takes his or her seat at the wedding banquet. We must keep the garment on until the bridegroom returns and the banquet begins. While Jesus is away, His disciples give the wedding robes to the guests as they enter the wedding banquet, the kingdom of heaven, by baptizing them:

---

[9] USCCB-NAB-Matt. 22:2-13, June 14, 2010. <www.usccb.org/nab/bible/matthew/matthew22.htm>

Go, therefore, and make disciples of all nations, baptizing them in the name of the Father, and of the Son, and of the holy Spirit, teaching them to observe all that I have commanded you.[10]

We decide to attend the wedding, and we decide to wear the wedding garment by choosing to follow God's commandments. During the erusin ceremony, the second blessing reminds us that we need to follow His commandments if we are to remain holy and betrothed:

Blessed are You, Lord our God, Master of the universe, Who has made us holy through His Commandments, and commanded us regarding illicit relations...

Our bridegroom repeatedly told us to show our love for Him by observing His commandments:

If you love me, you will keep my commandments.[11]

When Jesus returns for the wedding feast, we need to be wearing our wedding garment, we need to be living according to His teachings.

Like the ancient Jewish wedding, the coming of the Messiah is one intervention in human history, fulfilled in two stages. That is why Jesus' kingdom is here now on earth. That is why since the time of Jesus and the Apostles we are considered to be in the last days. That is why many of the prophecies about Jesus' coming apply to both the first and second Comings. They are speaking of both as one because from God's viewpoint, it is one intervention in human history.

Weddings are joyous occasions where love is palpable! Who doesn't enjoy a wedding? The wedding image is a beautiful one of love that perfectly illustrates God's relationship with His people. He is our Father, and He has sent His only Son to be our bridegroom so that He can take us unto Himself. Often called the people of God, we are more than that because weddings are about families. We are the children of God, the family of God, and it is a family formed in love.

---

[10] USCCB-NAB-Matthew 28:19-20
[11] USCCB-NAB-John 14:15, June 14, 2010. <www.usccb.org/nab/bible/john/john14.htm>

Blessed Mary reminds us of this in one of her recent messages at Medjugorje:

Dear children, today I call you to unity in Jesus, my Son. My motherly heart prays that you may comprehend that you are God's family... In discovering the Father, your life will be directed to the carrying out of God's will and the realization of God's family [12] *... Prayer will bring you to the fulfillment of my desire, of my mission here with you, to the unity in God's family.* [13]

As the bride must be faithful to the groom, we are called to be faithful to God. We do His will by following His commandments. Unfortunately, the scoffers miss this aspect of God's love for us, and don't believe He will come back for us, but the Holy Scriptures, our ketubah, proves otherwise. He came to forgive us and to save us, and will come again, because He loves us. The scoffers should not dwell on the wretchedness of this world. Instead, they should ponder the next, the perfect world prepared for His bride.

Jesus Himself promised He would return:

I am going away and I will come back to you. [14]

---

[12] "The Medjugorje Web – Apparitions of the Virgin Mary in Medjugorje", January 2, 2011. <www.medjugorje.org>

[13] Ibid, February 2, 2011.

[14] USCCB-NAB-John 14:28, June 14, 2010. <www.usccb.org/nab/bible/john/john14.htm>

Chapter 2
When Does the Bridegroom Return?

The Bible reveals God's plan of Salvation history and shows one intervention in two stages, following the ancient Jewish wedding ritual. The second stage is called the second coming of Jesus, and it will happen according to the Father's timeline. From the Bible, Revelation 20 provides a general outline:

> *Then I saw an angel come down from heaven, holding in his hand the key to the abyss and a heavy chain. He seized the dragon, the ancient serpent, which is the Devil or Satan, and tied it up for a thousand years... After this, it is to be released for a short time.... I also saw the souls of those who had been beheaded for their witness to Jesus and for the word of God, and who had not worshiped the beast or its image nor had accepted its mark on their foreheads or hands. They came to life and they reigned with Christ for a thousand years. The rest of the dead did not come to life until the thousand years were over ...*
>
> *When the thousand years are completed, Satan will be released from his prison. He will go out to deceive the nations at the four corners of the earth... to gather them for battle; their number is like the sand of the sea. They invaded the breadth of the earth and surrounded the camp of the holy ones and the beloved city. But fire came down from heaven and consumed them. The Devil who had led them astray was thrown into the pool of fire and sulfur, where the beast and the false prophet were. There they will be tormented day and night forever and ever.*

Next I saw a large white throne and the one who was sitting on it.... I saw the dead, the great and the lowly, standing before the throne... All the dead were judged according to their deeds... Anyone whose name was not found written in the book of life was thrown into the pool of fire. [15]

In brief, this passage says that for a long time, a figurative one thousand years, Satan will be restrained. He will still be able to try the Church, but he will not be able to prevent its spreading throughout the world. We know this because it speaks of martyrdom—those who had been beheaded—during the thousand years. Once released, Satan invades the breadth of the earth, which means that while confined, the word of God spread throughout the world. Released for a relatively short time, Satan manages to turn much of the world against the people of God. Finally, surrounded and facing defeat, the people of God are saved when He sends fire from heaven to consume Satan and his followers. They are cast into hell, and the dead rise and from His throne Christ judges all, according to their deeds.

The *Catechism of the Catholic Church* summarizes this:

Since the Ascension Christ's coming in glory has been imminent.... This eschatological coming could be accomplished at any moment, even if both it and the final trial that will precede it are "delayed."

Though already present in his Church, Christ's reign is nevertheless yet to be fulfilled "with power and great glory" by the king's return to earth. This reign is still under attack by the evil powers, even though they have been defeated definitively by Christ's Passover. Until everything is subject to him...the pilgrim Church, in her sacraments and institutions, which belong to this present age, carries the mark of this world which will pass, and she herself takes her place among the creatures which groan and travail yet and await the revelation of the sons of God.... [16]

---

[15] USCCB-NAB-Rev. 20:1-15, June 14, 2010. <www.usccb.org/nab/bible/revelation/revelation20.htm>
[16] *Catechism* **673,671.**

The figurative thousand years are granted to the Church guided by the Holy Spirit to spread the word of God throughout the world, while under attack from a restrained Satan:

> According to the Lord, the present time is the time of the Spirit and of witness, but also a time still marked by "distress" and the trial of evil which does not spare the Church and ushers in the struggles of the last days. It is a time of waiting and watching. [17]

Some theologians call the present time the Age of the Church.

Next, the catechism covers the Short Time of Satan's release just before the return of Christ. This final trial will result in an apostasy evidenced by man glorifying himself over God:

> Before Christ's second coming the Church must pass through a final trial that will shake the faith of many believers. The persecution that accompanies her pilgrimage on earth will unveil the "mystery of iniquity" in the form of a religious deception offering men an apparent solution to their problems at the price of apostasy from the truth. The supreme religious deception is that of the Antichrist, a pseudo-messianism by which man glorifies himself in place of God and of his Messiah come in the flesh.[18]

Finally, the catechism warns against believing Jesus will return and rule over the world while human history continues, albeit with God present in our midst to ensure righteousness:

> The Antichrist's deception already begins to take shape in the world every time the claim is made to realize within history that messianic hope which can only be realized beyond history through the eschatological judgment. The Church has rejected even modified forms of this falsification of the kingdom to come under the name of millenarianism, especially the "intrinsically perverse" political form of a secular messianism.

> The Church will enter the glory of the kingdom only through this final Passover, when she will follow her Lord in his death and

---

[17] *Catechism* 672.
[18] *Catechism* 675.

Resurrection. The kingdom will be fulfilled, then, not by a historic triumph of the Church through a progressive ascendancy, but only by God's victory over the final unleashing of evil… God's triumph over the revolt of evil will take the form of the Last Judgment after the final cosmic upheaval of this passing world.[19]

Graphically, a timeline for this is:

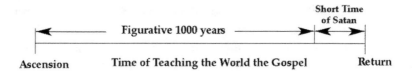

This presents a broad outline of the time between the bridegroom's ascension to His Father and His return to us.

From Scripture, we can fill in more details about the Short Time of Satan. Turning to the Olivet Discourse found in Matthew 24, we read:

And this gospel of the kingdom will be preached throughout the world as a witness to all nations, and then the end will come.[20]

Jesus is telling us what we already discovered in the Book of Revelation. The end—also called the end times, or as we have seen, the Short Time of Satan—comes after the disciples' preach the Gospel throughout the world. Jesus continues, giving a general description of the end times:

Jesus said to them in reply, "See that no one deceives you. For many will come in my name, saying, 'I am the Messiah,' and they will deceive many. You will hear of wars and reports of wars; see that you are not alarmed, for these things must happen, but it will not yet be the end. Nation will rise against nation, and kingdom against kingdom; there will be famines and earthquakes from place to place. All these are the beginning of the labor pains. Then they will hand you over to persecution, and they will kill you. You will be hated by all nations because of my name. And then many will be led into sin; they will betray and hate one another. Many false prophets will

---

[19] *Catechism* 676,677.
[20] USCCB-NAB-Matthew 24:14, June 14, 2010. <www.usccb.org/nab/bible/matthew/matthew24.htm>

arise and deceive many; and because of the increase of evildoing, the love of many will grow cold. But the one who perseveres to the end will be saved.[21]

False teachers will arise at the start and persist throughout the end times, both in and outside of the Church of Jesus. The Short Time of Satan will be marked by the constant threat of war, and notable famines and earthquakes in various places. Early on, war will erupt as nation rises against nation. This is the beginning of the birth pains. Birth in this context means the start of the next age upon the return of Jesus. After nation rises against nation, a brutal Christian persecution will begin. Then, their fellow leaders and teachers will lead many Christians into sin. This sinfulness of many Christians will dishearten others who will abandon the Gospel message of love of neighbor. Those who remain steadfast through all of the wars and reports of wars, the famines and earthquakes, the violent persecutions, the increase of evil and the betrayals of faith by their leaders and their friends, will be saved and enter into the next age. This provides a useful summary of what the end times will be like. Obviously, this Short Time of Satan must last for several years, and more likely for several decades, at the least.

Jesus next proceeds to break the Short Time of Satan into several sub-periods, placing these in sequential order.

For at that time there will be great tribulation, such as has not been since the beginning of the world until now, nor ever will be. And if those days had not been shortened, no one would be saved; but for the sake of the elect they will be shortened.[22]

This is the sub-period of great tribulation.

Immediately after the tribulation of those days, the sun will be darkened, and the moon will not give its light, and the stars will fall from the sky, and the powers of the heavens will be shaken.[23]

This is the sub-period of apostasy. The apostasy is a time when believers will fall away from their faith. Jesus' manner of speaking is confusing to us, but to His Jewish audience He was clear because Isaiah and other

---

[21] USCCB-NAB-Matthew 24:4-13
[22] USCCB-NAB-Matt. 24:21-22, June 14, 2010. <www.usccb.org/nab/bible/matthew/matthew24.htm>
[23] USCCB-NAB-Matthew 24:29

prophets used identical phrases (Isaiah 13:10 and 13:13, Ezekiel 32:7-8) to mean "the world will be turned upside down." The phrase was a Jewish idiom that meant political and spiritual upheaval. From Daniel chapter 12, the word stars in this context means spiritual leaders such as bishops, priests, and presbyters, or devoted disciples of Christ:

> *But they that are learned* [that is to say, learned in the law of God and true wisdom, which consists in knowing and loving God] *shall shine as the brightness of the firmament: and they that instruct many to justice, as stars for all eternity.*[24]

The shaking of the powers of the heavens means spiritual distress. Evil will spread and many Christians will lose their faith, and their spiritual leaders will fall into sin and error. Christ is the light of the world, but the loss of faith in Christ will bring darkness. During the Age of the Church, God's kingdom spreads and the number of Christian faithful increase. In the apostasy sub-period of the end times, many lose their faith.

> *And then the sign of the Son of Man will appear in heaven...*[25]

A sign, the nature of which has only recently become known, will appear in the sky after the sub-period of apostasy begins.

> *...and all the tribes of the earth will mourn...*[26]

At the appearance of the sign of the Son of Man, all people will know God's love and mercy. Knowing the end is near, they will lament their lives of unfaithfulness to God.

> *and they will see the Son of Man coming upon the clouds of heaven with power and great glory.*[27]

Jesus our bridegroom will return to claim His bride. At this point, the timeline of the Short Time of Satan looks like this:

---

[24] Douay-Rheims Bible, Prophecy of Daniel Chapter 12:3, with parenthetical explanation of *learned*, from same source, added. May 31, 2010. <www.drbo.org/chapter/32012.htm>
[25] USCCB-NAB-Matt. 24:30a, June 14, 2010. <www.usccb.org/nab/bible/matthew/matthew24.htm>
[26] USCCB-NAB-Matt. 24:30b
[27] USCCB-NAB-Matt. 24:30c

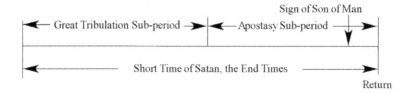

While the graphical representation shows a clear distinction between the end of the great tribulation and the start of the apostasy, the boundary between the two sub-periods blurs, with cruel persecutions continuing into the time of the apostasy, and apostatizing events occurring towards the end of the great tribulation. The first period flows into the next. The *Catechism of the Catholic Church* speaks of a final persecution that leads to an apostasy:

> Before Christ's second coming the Church must pass through a final [persecution] that will … unveil…a religious deception offering men an apparent solution to their problems at the price of apostasy from the truth.[28]

Scripture mentions a final trial broken into sub-periods in books other than Matthew. Daniel chapter 12 says:

> *…and a time shall come such as never was from the time that nations began even until that time…And I said…How long shall it be to the end of these wonders?… And I heard… that it should be unto a time, and times, and half a time.*[29]

The Short Time of Satan is described as lasting for a "time, and times, and half a time". To understand this, we need to look at the Hebrew language. Hebrew has three numbers for nouns. Like English, it has singular and plural. Additionally, Hebrew has a dual, which means "a pair of." The Hebrew word for ear is "ozen," the plural ears is "ozniym" and a pair of ears is "oznayim". In Daniel 12 the word times in the expression "time, and times and half a time" is the dual "mo'edayim". The expression "time, and times, and half a time" means three and a half units of time. This breaks the Short Time of Satan into sub-periods. Additionally, it sets the proportion of each of the three sub-periods—it gives ratios to each of

---

[28] *Catechism* 675.
[29] Douay-Rheims Bible, Prophecy of Daniel Chapter 12:1,6-7

them, setting the duration of each sub-period with respect to the others. The ratio can be expressed as 1:2:0.5, or, 1 to 2 to 0.5. Previously, we had identified two sub-periods within the Short Time of Satan. From Matthew 24, we know the apostasy comes immediately after the great tribulation, and just before the return of Jesus. This means the additional sub-period must come before the great tribulation. Our timeline becomes:

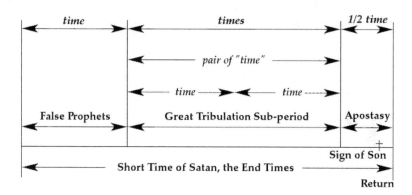

At this point, details about the end times period that occurs just before the arrival of the bridegroom are clearer.

Summarizing what we have discovered so far:

- Mirroring the two stages of a Jewish wedding, Jesus came once to complete the first stage, and as our bridegroom, He will come a second time to consummate the marriage between God and His people.
- A careful reading of Scripture reveals a general timeline for the return of Jesus.
- After the Ascension, the Church spreads around the world under the guidance of the Holy Spirit. This is the age of the Church, the figurative one thousand years of growth before the Short Time of Satan.
- During the age of the Church, the Gospel is preached to all nations.

- The Short Time of Satan, also known as the end times, consists of three distinguishable periods that run consecutively:
    - a period of false teachings before the Great Tribulation;
    - the Great Tribulation, which is cut short;
    - the apostasy.
- War will be a consistent characteristic of the end times. When nations are not openly warring, the threat of war will persist until the next open conflict.
- Notable famines and earthquakes will occur from time to time in various places.
- Signs and wonders will occur during the end times.
- The sign of the Son of man will appear shortly before Jesus returns.

Chapter 3
Can We Know When He Returns?

While we have discovered a general timeline that describes the Short Time of Satan, it does not reveal when this Short Time of Satan begins. It ends with the return of Jesus, but He said no man would know when He returns:

> *But of that day and hour no one knows, neither the angels of heaven, nor the Son, but the Father alone.*[30]

Jesus is very specific. Of the day and the hour, none will know. Hindsight is always more successful than foresight in determining Bible prophecy. Obviously, this presents a dilemma for studying end times prophecies because there will be no hindsight. However, Jesus said there would be signs that will provide enough foresight to help us know His return is near:

> *In the same way, when you see all these things, know that he is near, at the gates.*[31]

In addition, in the Old Testament, we read:

---

[30] USCCB-NAB-Matt. 24:36, June 14, 2010. <www.usccb.org/nab/bible/matthew/matthew24.htm>
[31] USCCB-NAB-Matt. 24:33

Indeed, the Lord GOD does nothing without revealing his plan to his servants, the prophets.[32]

Throughout Scripture, by way of His prophets, God warns that His wrath is about to come upon the people. After saying the Father alone knew of His return, Jesus compared the end time to the days of Noah:

For as it was in the days of Noah, so it will be at the coming of the Son of Man.[33]

Noah was one such prophet who warned the people that God was about to inflict punishment. In the New Testament, Peter reminds us that Noah was a herald of righteousness:

And if he did not spare the ancient world, even though he preserved Noah, a herald of righteousness, together with seven others, when he brought a flood upon the godless world...[34]

God sent Jonah to Nineveh's inhabitants to warn them to repent of their evil ways because the wrath of God was about to come upon them. Recall that Moses warned Egypt, and Isaiah warned Israel. There are many others. The last and greatest prophet of the Bible, John the Baptist, warned the people of Israel to repent because the kingdom of heaven was at hand. Just as Noah preached righteousness to the people and warned them of the coming judgment of God, before the return of the Son of Man we can expect a messenger.

In fact, Jesus explicitly said a messenger of righteousness would precede His Second Coming:

Then the disciples asked him, "Why do the scribes say that Elijah must come first?" He said in reply, "Elijah will indeed come and restore all things; but I tell you that Elijah has already come, and they did not recognize him but did to him whatever they pleased. So also will the Son of Man suffer at their hands."

Then the disciples understood that he was speaking to them of John the Baptist.[35]

[32] USCCB-NAB-Amos 3:7, June 15, 2010. < www.usccb.org/nab/bible/amos/amos3.htmm>
[33] USCCB-NAB-Matt. 24:37, June 14, 2010. <www.usccb.org/nab/bible/matthew/matthew24.htm>
[34] USCCB-NAB-2 Pet. 2:5, June 14, 2010. <www.usccb.org/nab/bible/2peter/2peter2.htm>
[35] USCCB-NAB-Matt. 17:10-13

Jesus indicates Elijah will come before the Son of Man returns, but by referencing John the Baptist, He also makes it clear it is not Elijah who is to come but one like Elijah. Here Jesus makes use of typology, an important tool used throughout the ages by Biblical scholars to interpret Sacred Scriptures. Typology will be discussed in more detail, but briefly, the Bible reveals that John the Baptist preached repentance with the spirit and power of the Old Testament prophet Elijah (Luke 1:13-17). The "Elijah" who will come and restore all things will be someone who also preaches repentance and righteousness with the spirit and power of Elijah.

God sends prophets who warn of His impending wrath, and in most cases, the time when it will occur is given, too. To Noah, God said:

Seven days from now I will bring rain down on the earth for forty days and forty nights, and so I will wipe out from the surface of the earth every moving creature that I have made.[36]

God spoke through the prophet Jonah to the city of Nineveh:

Jonah began his journey through the city, and had gone but a single day's walk announcing, "Forty days more and Nineveh shall be destroyed."[37]

Moses warned the Pharaoh of Egypt about a plague, and gave him the time it would occur:

"But the LORD will distinguish between the livestock of Israel and that of Egypt, so that none belonging to the Israelites will die." And setting a definite time, the LORD added, "Tomorrow the LORD shall do this in the land." And on the next day the LORD did so.[38]

While we cannot know the exact day and hour of Christ's return, Scripture makes it clear that we will be given not only signs, but also a messenger who heralds His approach. Most likely, the messenger will also point toward a general timeframe for the return of the Bridegroom.

---

[36] USCCB-NAB-Genesis 7:4, June 15, 2010. <www.usccb.org/nab/bible/genesis/genesis7.htm>

[37] USCCB-NAB-Jonah 3:4, June 15, 2010. <www.usccb.org/nab/bible/jonah/jonah3.htm>

[38] USCCB-NAB-Exodus 9:4-6, June 15, 2010. <www.usccb.org/nab/bible/exodus/exodus9.htm>

Chapter 4
And The World Turned

Adam and Eve fell. Inexorably, God's plan for the restoration of mankind unfolded, and after thousands of years of prophets, Malachi[39] spoke to the people of God about one who would herald the coming of the Lord:

> *Lo, I am sending my messenger to prepare the way before me...Lo, I will send you Elijah, the prophet, Before the day of the LORD comes...to turn the hearts of the fathers to their children, and the hearts of the children to their fathers*[40]

Still, God remained silent for another 400 years, but then, according to His own timeline, He intervened in human history by sending an angel to Zechariah to announce the birth of the messenger spoken of in Malachi:

> *But the angel said to him, "Do not be afraid, Zechariah, because your prayer has been heard. Your wife Elizabeth will bear you a son, and you shall name him John...he will go before him in the spirit and power of Elijah to turn the hearts of fathers toward children and the disobedient to the understanding of the righteous, to prepare a people fit for the Lord."* [41]

---

[39] Book of Malachi, last book of the Old Testament.
[40] USCCB-NAB-Mal. 3:1,23-24, June 15, 2010. <www.usccb.org/nab/bible/malachi/malachi3.htm>
[41] USCCB-NAB-Luke 1:13,17

Between the first and second parts of her wedding, the angel Gabriel appeared to Mary and asked her to be the mother of the Son of God. About thirty-three years later, Mary's Son and our bridegroom would atone for our sins on the cross and then rise from the dead.

Forty days after rising from the dead, Jesus returned to His Father's house, but the ketubah, the Holy Scriptures, remains with His bride, the Church. The ketubah, the Jewish wedding contract, states what the groom shall do for his bride. In the Sacred Scriptures, Jesus promises eternal life to everyone who remains faithful to Him, a faith demonstrated by our actions.

In the Acts of the Apostles, we read of the disciples' efforts to baptize and to teach the nations all that Jesus commanded them (Matthew 28:20). The Apostles, acting as the first bishops, established churches throughout the Mediterranean. Peter and Paul died in Rome in the early 60s CE. James reached Spain, and tradition holds that doubting Thomas was martyred in southern India. Matthew is thought to have been martyred in Ethiopia, while Bartholomew was martyred in Armenia for his preaching. The Apostles and their disciples preached throughout the Mediterranean basin, into Armenia and Babylonia, reaching as far as India in the east, and Spain in the west. John, the last Apostle, wrote the Book of Revelation while in exile on the island of Patmos before returning to spend his final days in Ephesus. Even with his last words, "little children, love one another," John obediently taught the Gospel message of Jesus.

By the second century, there were many established bishoprics within the Roman Empire including Northern Africa, present day France, Italy, Syria, Greece, and Turkey, in addition to twenty bishoprics outside the empire, mainly in Armenia. The Catholic Church suffered many trials throughout the first several centuries, culminating with the last, greatest, and bloodiest persecution ordered by Emperor Diocletian in 303 CE. The persecution did not destroy the empire's Catholic community, and in 313, Emperor Constantine ended the persecutions with the Edict of Milan. In 380, the Edict of Thessalonica made Catholicism the official state religion of the Roman Empire.

In the fifth century, Catholic missionaries spread the Gospel from Roman Britain into present day Scotland, Ireland, and Wales. In Gaul (modern France), Frankish King Clovis converted in 496. In the seventh century, Catholic missionaries brought the teaching of Christ to the Germanic peoples and into the present day Netherlands regions. By 800, Western Europe was ruled entirely by Christian kings. In the ninth century missionaries reached modern Denmark and into Sweden and Norway, and in the ninth and tenth centuries the Gospel was brought to the Ukraine, Belarus, Russia, Bulgaria, and Serbia.

In central Asia, Pope Nicholas III established the Diocese of Kepciak, Kazakhstan in 1278. Italian Franciscan missionary John of Montecorvino brought Catholicism to the Mongols in the early 1300s and translated the New Testament and Psalms into Chinese. The Portuguese established churches in Malacca after conquering it in 1511.

In the late fifteenth century, explorers brought Catholicism to the Americas. During the sixteenth century, missionaries spread across the Caribbean to Mexico, Central America, parts of South America, and the American Southwest. Around 1550, serious Catholic missionary activity began in Japan. The Philippines received the Gospel message starting in 1565 when the first Spanish colonies were established. In 1576, Pope Gregory XIII authorized the creation of the Roman Catholic Diocese of Macau. Jesuits arrived in China in 1574, reestablishing a Christian foothold in that land. Catholics arrived in Australia in 1788, and the first priests arrived in 1800. Starting in the 1830s, the Marists brought Catholicism to Oceania. In 1868, the Society of Missionaries of Africa, popularly known as the White Fathers because of their white tunics, was founded to evangelize Africa. The society began missionary work in northern Algeria. Ten years later, its members had reached as far as the Rift Valley lakes region of East Africa, founding Catholic missions in the area. By 1895, the society extended its work to western Africa. In 1900, a mission station was established in Rwanda, one of the last areas of Africa to receive Christian missionaries, so that by the start of the twentieth century the Gospel message had been preached throughout the world.

It is important to note that Jesus did not say all nations and peoples would convert to Catholicism or even to Christianity before the end comes. He said:

And this gospel of the kingdom will be preached throughout the world as a witness to all nations, and then the end will come.[42]

Jesus also clearly indicated that not all those who heard the Gospel would accept it:

Then he summoned the Twelve and began to send them out in pairs ... 'And if any place does not welcome you and people refuse to listen to you, as you

---

[42] USCCB-NAB-Mat. 24:14, June 17, 2010. <www.usccb.org/nab/bible/matthew/matthew24.htm>

walk away shake off the dust under your feet as evidence to them.' So they set off to proclaim repentance. [43]

Inexorably, the Gospel teachings of Jesus were preached to all peoples. Throughout the centuries, as civilizations came and went and empires rose and fell, the ebb and flow of its influence on world history is evident. As the age of the Church draws to a close, the promise made to Abraham long ago nears its fulfillment:

I will bless you abundantly and make your descendants as countless as the stars of the sky and the sands of the seashore...in your descendants all the nations of the earth shall find blessing. [44]

---

[43] Catholic Online, Mat. 6:7,11, June 14, 2010. <www.catholic.org/bible/book.php?id=53>
[44] USCCB-NAB-Genesis 22:17-18

Chapter 5
Reading the Ketubah

The ketubah, the Holy Scriptures, influenced Jesus' bride, His chosen, throughout the centuries but His people longed for the signs of His return and for the Elijah who is to come and restore all things. While waiting for the groom's return, we have the ketubah to read and re-read. The Holy Scriptures is our marriage contract. It is tangible proof of God's love for us, and holds the promise of His return.

The traditional Jewish wedding contract explains the groom's obligation to provide for a faithful bride. It is a contract from the groom to the betrothed to honor, support, and maintain her in truth; to provide food, clothing and necessities.

> So do not worry and say, 'What are we to eat?' or 'What are we to drink?' or 'What are we to wear?'...Your heavenly Father knows that you need them all.[45]

After the betrothal, the groom departs, but the ketubah remains with the bride. Before Jesus returned to His Father, He promised to send the Holy Spirit to His disciples to maintain them in truth:

> The Advocate, the holy Spirit —he will teach you everything and remind you of all that (I) told you.[46] ..., he will guide you to all truth.[47]

---

[45] USCCB-NAB-Matthew 6:31-32, 26; June 17, 2010. <usccb.org/nab/bible/matthew/matthew6.htm>
[46] USCCB-NAB-John 14:15-17,26

The disciples began to build up His Church on the very day the Holy Spirit came upon them during the feast of Pentecost.

Maintained in truth given to them by the Holy Spirit from the days after Jesus left until the end of the age, the disciples and their successors in an unbroken line of bishops are the ones who preserve and interpret the ketubah, the Holy Scriptures. The teaching authority of the Church interprets the Holy Scriptures; the Bible itself warns against personal interpretations:

> *Know this first of all, that there is no prophecy of scripture that is a matter of personal interpretation, for no prophecy ever came through human will; but rather human beings moved by the holy Spirit spoke under the influence of God.*[48]

The Church, the bride of Christ, understands and interprets the teachings of Christ on matters of faith and morals. By following the Gospel, we remain faithful to our groom.

The Catholic Church explains how to read the Holy Scriptures. The *Catechism of the Catholic Church* speaks of two senses in Scripture: the literal sense and the spiritual sense. The spiritual sense, in turn, is made up of three kinds: the allegorical (or "typological" sense), the moral, and the anagogical (or "heavenly") sense. Thus, Scripture has two "natures": a literal meaning and a spiritual meaning. We might summarize it this way:

> The literal sense of Scripture is the meaning conveyed by the words, discovered through sound interpretation. All other senses of Scripture are based on the literal.

> From the typological sense, we can acquire a more profound understanding of events by recognizing their significance in Christ; thus the crossing of the Red Sea is a sign or type of Christ's victory and also of Christian Baptism.

> The moral sense of the Old Testament moves the Christian to act justly in the life of the Church by instructing us how to act or behave.

---

[47] USCCB-NAB-John 16:13
[48] USCCB-NAB-2 Peter 1:20-21

The anagogical sense means we can view realities and events in terms of their eternal significance, leading us toward our true homeland: thus the Church on earth is a sign of the heavenly Jerusalem.

The *Catechism of the Catholic Church* says, "the economy of the Old Testament was deliberately so oriented that it should prepare for and declare in prophecy the coming of Christ, redeemer of all men."[49]

It is not just the Old Testament that prefigures the New; some New Testament passages serve as types for other New Testament passages. For example, the Gospels of the New Testament relate the passion, death, and resurrection of Jesus. Later, in the twelfth chapter of the Book of Acts, we see how this prefigured Peter's imprisonment. Jesus' body was placed in the tomb on the day after the Passover meal, and soldiers guarded that tomb. On the Feast of Unleavened Bread, which occurs on the day after the Passover meal, Herod had Peter arrested and thrown into prison, under guard of four squads of soldiers. Jesus died on the cross, between two thieves. In prison on the night before he was to be taken before Herod, Peter slept between two guards. Jesus rose from the dead, and an angel rolled back the stone that sealed the tomb. An angel appeared to Peter, unlocked his chains, and opened the prison doors. Women came to the tomb and found it empty, and were told Jesus had risen. Finally, Mary recognizes Jesus by His voice, and after speaking to her, Jesus departs to go to His Father. Later when the women told the disciples, they were not believed. Rhoda, the maid, recognized Peter's voice when he spoke to her through the door and told the others Peter had arrived, but she was not believed. Peter continued to knock until they finally opened the door. After speaking to them, he left for another place.

What happened to Jesus is a type for what later happened to Peter. This teaches how Peter, as the holder of the keys, acts in the person of Jesus, rather than in name only. One title of the pope is the Vicar of Christ, meaning the one who acts in the person of Christ. From this it follows that all bishops and priests who remain obedient to the pope also act in the person of Christ.

Typology

In typology, a type is a person, event, or thing in the Old Testament that prefigures or symbolizes some future reality that God brings to pass.

---

[49] *Catechism* 116,117,122.

In Biblical exegesis, typology is a tool used to explain and investigate the relationship between the Old and New Testaments. Persons, events, and objects in the Old Testament are seen as prefiguring persons, events or objects in the New Testament, especially regarding the central figure of Christ. In this way, the Old Testament comes to its purpose and reaches its fulfillment in the New Testament. Persons, events, or objects in the Old Testament are called "types" that prefigure "antitypes" in the New Testament. Typology is not limited to type-antitype relationships across testaments, however; persons, events, or objects in the New Testament, for example, can prefigure other persons, events, or objects of the New Testament.

From the *Catechism of the Catholic Church*:

> The Church, as early as apostolic times, and then constantly in her Tradition, has illuminated the unity of the divine plan in the two Testaments through typology, which discerns in God's works of the Old Covenant pre-figurations of what He accomplished in the fullness of time in the person of His incarnate Son.

> Christians therefore read the Old Testament in the light of Christ crucified and risen. Such typological reading discloses the inexhaustible content of the Old Testament; but it must not make us forget that the Old Testament retains its own intrinsic value as Revelation reaffirmed by our Lord himself...Early Christian catechesis made constant use of the Old Testament. As an old saying put it, "the New Testament lies hidden in the Old and the Old Testament is unveiled in the New".

> Typology indicates the dynamic movement toward the fulfillment of the divine plan when "God [will] be everything to everyone." [50]

Some examples of typology are:

> Abraham's near-sacrifice of his only son Isaac on an altar, as willed by God, is seen as a prefiguring of God the Father sacrificing His only Son Jesus on the altar of the cross. Instead of sacrificing his son, God had Abraham stop, and then substituted a sacrifice He Himself

---

[50] *Catechism* 128-130.

provided—a ram (male sheep, prefiguring Jesus, the lamb of God) found with its horns stuck in a thicket (prefiguring the crown of thorns of Jesus).

Moses is a type for Christ. He led the people of God out of bondage in Egypt into the Promised Land, while Jesus leads the people of God out of the bondage of sin and into the promised land of heaven.

Objects can be types as well. God dwelled within the Ark of the Covenant which contained the Ten Commandments, the Word of God on stone tablets; a pot with manna, which is bread that came down from heaven; and Aaron's staff. God dwelled within Blessed Mary in the person of Jesus Who is the Word of God in the flesh. Jesus said He is the living manna come down from heaven. Aaron's staff came back to life when it budded, and the rod signified Aaron was the high priest. Jesus came back to life and He is our High Priest. Therefore typologically Mary is sometimes called the Ark of the New Covenant.

Jesus connected the prophet Elijah to John the Baptist. The Jews had been expecting the actual Elijah to return to herald the coming of the Messiah, but Jesus told the disciples that John the Baptist was "Elijah". And Jesus also said another "Elijah" will come before He returns. So Jesus makes it clear Elijah was a type for John the Baptist, as well as the "Elijah" to come.

Other specific examples of types: Adam was a type of Christ (Rom. 5:14); Noah's Ark and the Flood were types of the Church and baptism (1 Peter 3:19-21); the Passover lamb in Exodus 12:21-28 was a symbol of Jesus, the Lamb of God, slain on the Cross to save sinners. Death passed over the houses marked with the blood of a lamb on the door beams. The Jewish slaves went through that door into the Promised Land. The blood of Jesus on wooden beams in the form of a cross freed us from death. *"No one comes to the Father except through me."*[51] The crucified Christ becomes the doorway into Heaven, which had been closed to mankind since the original sin of Adam and Eve. We go through that doorway and journey from bondage to sin into the promised paradise of heaven.

Since Jesus ascended into heaven we have been living in the last days. We are living under the New Covenant. Until salvation history is fulfilled at His return, it is possible for historical events to have typological meanings.

---

[51] USCCB-NAB-John 14:6, June 12, 2010. <www.usccb.org/nab/bible/john/john14.htm>

The end of the Old Covenant is a historical event that seems to be a type for the fulfillment of the New Covenant, which happens at the end of the age. It is in the New Covenant that Jesus brings about the promise to Abraham that in his descendents all the nations of the earth shall find blessing. But the audience of the Old Covenant was the Jewish people. The scope of the Old Covenant is Jerusalem and the Mediterranean world, most of which became part of the Roman Empire by the time of Jesus. At that time, the small camp of holy people and the holy city of Jerusalem worshipping the one true God stood alone against the pagan onslaught of the Roman world. In 66 CE, thirty-three years after the death of Jesus, the first Roman-Jewish war ignited and three and a half years later Roman legions besieged Jerusalem, entered the Holy of Holies and burned the Temple and much of the city, and killed or enslaved upwards of one million Jews. The Christians in Jerusalem at that time managed to escape to Pella. Dying Jews saw the Temple on fire. In the days that followed, as the surviving Jews were rounded up to be sent into slavery, they witnessed the Roman pagans tearing down the Temple, the house where the one true God dwelt, stone by stone. Jewish life revolved around the Temple and its destruction along with the slaughter of so many was a time of great tribulation for the Jews.

The fulfillment of the New Covenant will be like the end of the Old, but this time the scope will be worldwide. The Gospel message of Jesus has spread around the world, creating the "City of God". Since the twentieth century, the people of God have been under siege both physically and spiritually, in a unique way[52]. Just as the pagan empire of Rome surrounded the holy people who worshipped the one true God, and their holy city of Jerusalem, so now the holy people of the city of God throughout the world are surrounded and oppressed by non-believers. Already we see Christians pushed from the public square, public schools, and from the halls of government. Anti-Christian practices such as abortion, gay marriage, and euthanasia are now being codified into law in Europe and the US, both former bastions of Christianity. During the age of

---

[52] While other times saw religions pitted against one another, such as Jews versus Christians, Christians versus pagan gods, and Muslims versus Christians, in the twentieth century godless men took power over large swaths of the Christian world and tried to end all religion, to "convert" entire nations to atheism, and to make man the supreme ruler of all things. This happened when the ideological movement known as communism was put into practice, starting in Russia. And while the brutal physical persecution of adherents to Christianity and other religions have mostly come to an end, holdover anti-religious ideas of atheism, moral relativism, modernism and others are actually gaining ground in once pre-dominantly Christian regions.

the Church, Christian principles influenced Western governments. Today, the gains made over two thousand years are being eroded, especially in regions that were the first to adopt Christianity. In those regions many make a pretense of religion. Paul warns about people in the last days who go through the form or ritual of religion without any inner change, no evidence of Christ dwelling in them. All Christians in Jerusalem at the time of the end of the Old Covenant survived the pagan Roman onslaught, entered into the New Covenant, and started the age of the Church. Will true Christians in the city of God that exists throughout the world today survive to see the fulfillment of the New Covenant and enter into the new heaven and the new earth? Our ketubah promises us that the Church founded by Jesus will survive to the end of the age and we will be saved, provided we remain faithful to our Groom.

The destruction of Jerusalem in 70 CE ended the time of the Old Covenant and is a major event in salvation history that serves as a type for the fulfillment of the Church age, commonly called the end of the world. Jesus gave the description of this in Matthew 24 to serve as a type for future events in salvation history. From our timeline, we see it described as an era when false teachings come to the fore, followed by great persecution that leads to apostasy. Finally, the sign of the son of man appears in the sky.

In fact, events similar to those described by Jesus occurred in the late third and early fourth centuries. The late third century witnessed the rise of the Arianism heresy. The Arian concept of Christ denies that the Son is of one essence with God and posits the Son of God did not always exist, but was created by God the Father and therefore is not His equal, and not a real Deity. This false teaching involved many church members from simple believers to priests and monks as well as bishops, emperors and members of Rome's imperial family, and was one of the most pervasive heresies to ever threaten the existence of Christ's Church.

Many false prophets will arise and deceive many.[53]

While this false teaching festered throughout the empire, persecution of Christians began in earnest in early 303CE when Roman Emperor Diocletian issued his first edict against Christians. This edict ordered the destruction of Christian churches and the burning of Scriptures and liturgical books, and placed a ban on the Mass. Christians also were denied

---

[53] USCCB-NAB-Matthew 24:11, June 14, 2010. <www.usccb.org/nab/bible/matthew/matthew24.htm>

their right to petition in the Roman courts and those serving in the government and the military were stripped of their ranks and titles, and Christian soldiers lost their state pensions. The second edict, issued in the summer of 303, ordered the arrest and imprisonment of all Christian clergy, including bishops, priests, deacons, and lectors (readers). In the fall, a third edict promised any imprisoned clergy who offered sacrifice to Rome's pagan gods would be set free. Early in 304, Diocletian issued the final edict, ordering all men, women and children to gather in public places and offer sacrifices to the pagan gods, under pain of death.[54] Unable to offer sacrifice to false gods, over the next ten years thousands of Christian men, women, and children were tortured and executed for their faith. This time is known today in Church history as the Great Persecution.

Then they will hand you over to persecution, and they will kill you.[55]

The third edict was geared toward fracturing the Christian community by publicly showing clergy members apostatizing by sacrificing to the pagan gods. Already happening because of Arianism, apostasy increased because of the persecutions. Historian Eusebius of Caesarea reported the four edicts resulted in innumerable apostates from the faith. Among these were many clergy, the stars of the Church.

Many will be led into sin; they will betray and hate one another… and because of the increase of evildoing, the love of many will grow cold. …Immediately after the tribulation of those days, the sun will be darkened, and the moon will not give its light, and the stars will fall from the sky, and the powers of the heavens will be shaken.

During the reign of Diocletian, the Roman Empire was split into four territories, each headed by its own emperor. By 312, Emperor Maxentius of the western sector that included Rome, and Emperor Constantine, ruler of Spain and Gaul, were openly hostile to one another, and Constantine decided to remove Maxentius. In the fall, he marched against him. On 27 October 312, the day before the two armies clashed at the Milvian Bridge that led into Rome, Constantine had a vision. Historian Eusebius became a confidante of Constantine in his later years and reported that Constantine

---

[54] YouTube – History of Christianity 4: Trials and Triumphs, June 22, 2010. <www.youtube.com/watch?v=HpOa8kveuqQ>

[55] USCCB-NAB-Matthew 24:9, June 14, 2010. <www.usccb.org/nab/bible/matthew/matthew24.htm>

described the vision as a cross-like symbol above the sun, accompanied by the words, "In this sign, conquer."

> And then the sign of the Son of Man will appear in heaven [meaning in the sky]...[56]

Constantine also said Jesus appeared to him in a dream that night and said he should have his soldiers put the sign he had seen in the sky on their shields to defend them in battle. They did, and the next day, outnumbered two to one, Constantine's army was victorious and Maxentius was killed. In 313, Constantine together with Licinius, ruler of the eastern empire, issued the Edict of Milan that proclaimed religious toleration in the Roman Empire. Christian churches and other properties were returned. Constantine became sole emperor a few years later, and under his rule, Christianity became the dominant religion in the empire. In 380, under the Edict of Thessalonica, Catholicism became the official religion of the Roman Empire. Pagan Rome crucified Christ, martyred Peter and Paul, and destroyed the Temple, ending the Old Covenant, but by the end of the fourth century, the teachings of Jesus had triumphed over the known "world", the Roman Empire.

The conversion of the Roman world is an antitype to the Olivet Discourse. Viewed through the eyes of salvation history, it is also a typological preview for what will happen at the end of the age—false teachers, persecution, apostasy, the sign of the Son of Man in the sky, and finally, the arrival of the Bridegroom, followed by the wedding feast.

Summarizing:

- While we cannot know the exact day and hour of our Bridegroom's return, signs and a messenger in the spirit and power of Elijah will be given beforehand to help us know His approach is near.
- Around the start of the twentieth century, the Gospel had been preached throughout the world.
- The ketubah, the Holy Scriptures, is kept by the bride, which is the Church, who reads it and interprets it, along with Sacred Tradition, under the guidance of the Holy Spirit, to understand

---

[56] USCCB-NAB-Matt. 24:30a, June 14, 2010. <www.usccb.org/nab/bible/matthew/matthew24.htm>

how to remain faithful to our Groom while we await His return.

- The Bible is written and interpreted in both the literal and spiritual sense. One kind of spiritual sense is typology, which helps us to see salvation history through world history. Often, historical events related to salvation history serve as previews or types for future events in salvation history.

- The Short Time of Satan is the period before the fulfillment of the New Covenant at the end of the age. The last days of the Old Covenant, described by Jesus in the Olivet Discourse, serve as a type or preview for this short time and set the pattern for it, as shown in our timeline.

- The events surrounding the conversion of the Roman Empire in the fourth century are an antitype to the end of the Old Covenant described by Jesus in the Olivet Discourse. They too fit the pattern of the end times we see in our timeline—false teachings, great persecution and apostasy, followed by the sign of the Son of Man in the sky.

- The conversion of the Roman world to Christianity is an antitype to the end of the Old Covenant, but it also serves as a type for a future event in salvation history. It is a type for the end of this present world, for the end times which will follow the same pattern of false teachings, great persecution, apostasy, the sign of the Son of Man in the sky, and finally, the return of Jesus. The triumph of Christianity over the Roman Empire previews the triumph of Christ over the entire world with His return at the end of the age.

- Because the events surrounding the end of the Roman Empire so closely fit our timeline for the end times, it is clear that in Matthew 24 Jesus was not only talking about the end of the Old Covenant, but He was speaking typologically about the Short Time of Satan at the end of this present world.

Chapter 6
The Second Part of the Jewish Wedding

After the prophecies of Malachi, four hundred years passed before an angel appeared to Zechariah as the first event in the first coming of the Messiah. Two thousand years after Jesus returned to His Father and His teachings had spread throughout the world, Heaven directly interjected itself into world history again in a visible manner, in accordance with God's timeline for the salvation of man.

This occurred in 1917 at a place near Fatima, Portugal, when it was reported by three young shepherd children that Blessed Mary had appeared to them. Beginning on 13 May 1917 Our Lady appeared six times, the last apparition occurring on 13 October 1917. This last date is of great significance. Blessed Mary promised a miracle would happen on that day as a sign so an estimated 70,000 people came from far and wide to witness it. They were not disappointed. What they saw that day has become known as the Miracle of the Sun. Those present were able to look at the sun without damaging their eyes. They saw the sun spin and whirl as it gave off many colors —the popular expression for it is 'the sun danced'. Then the fiery sun appeared to break free from its moorings in the sky and plunged to the earth, terrifying the onlookers. Finally, it receded back to its original place.

The apparition of Our Lady at Fatima is the most important event in salvation history since the time of the Apostles so it will be explored fully. Before this event though, there were other more private indications of 'things to come'. Church history is dotted with apparitions of Blessed Mary and other saints, and even visits by Jesus from time to time. In the majority of cases these do not occur to the princes of the Church, the bishops, but to humble people of strong faith. It is an exceptional event when a report of a vision comes from the Vicar of Christ, the head of the Church on earth.

For years rumors circulated that Pope Pius XII, who reigned from 1939 to 1958, had seen Fatima's Miracle of the Sun repeated at the Vatican. He told a few cardinals and his closest collaborators but did not speak of it publicly. The only indirect acknowledgement came in a homily given by Cardinal Federico Tedeschini.[57] However in November 2008, a handwritten unpublished note from Pope Pius XII confirmed it.[58] Pius XII's note says that he saw the miracle in the year he was to proclaim the dogma of the Assumption of Blessed Mary, 1950, while he walked in the Vatican Gardens. He said he saw the phenomenon four times and considered it a confirmation of his plan to declare the dogma.[59]

> The papal note says that at 4 p.m. on 30 October 1950, during his "habitual walk in the Vatican Gardens, reading and studying," having arrived to the statue of Our Lady of Lourdes, "toward the top of the hill...I was awestruck by a phenomenon that before now I had never seen."

> "The sun, which was still quite high, looked like a pale, opaque sphere, entirely surrounded by a luminous circle...the opaque sphere moved outward slightly, either spinning, or moving from left to right and vice versa. But within the sphere, you could see marked movements with total clarity and without interruption," he recounted. And one could look at the sun, "without the slightest bother."... Pius XII said he saw the same phenomenon "the 31st of October and Nov. 1, the day of the definition of the dogma of the Assumption, and then again Nov. 8, and after that, no more."[60]

Interestingly, Pope Benedict XV ordained Pius XII a bishop on 13 May 1917, the date of the first apparition of Our Lady of Fatima.

---

[57] ZENIT – Pius XII Saw 'Miracle of the Sun', "Handwritten Note Reveals Pope's Experience", Antonio Gaspari, retrieved June 25, 2010. <www.zenit.org/article-24149?l=english >
[58] Ibid.
[59] Ibid.
[60] Ibid.

All of this is to say as with any institution, rumors, truths and half-truths circulate within the walls of the Vatican. What makes Pius XII's story of his seeing the Miracle of the Sun unique is that after more than half a century of rumors written proof was finally discovered. But hints of other unsubstantiated rumors persist, and one of these is of particular interest.

Reportedly on 13 October 1884, Pope Leo XIII saw a horrifying vision in the sixth year of his pontificate, at the age of seventy-four. After the Pontiff celebrated mass in his private Vatican Chapel, attended by a few cardinals and members of the Vatican staff, he suddenly stopped at the foot of the altar and collapsed to the floor in a deep trance, his face gray. Physicians who rushed to his side feared he had already died because they could not find a pulse. After about ten minutes the Holy Father recovered. Opening his eyes, he emotionally announced he had been permitted to see a horrible vision. In this vision, God gave Satan the choice of one century in which to submit the Church to his worst persecutions and the devil chose the twentieth century. Moved by this prophetic vision of the coming century of sorrow and war, the Holy Father immediately went from the chapel to his office where he composed the prayer to St. Michael the Archangel, giving instructions that it be said after all low masses throughout the world.

While not confirmed, the story has stayed very much alive within the walls of the Vatican. Pope John Paul II alluded to it while speaking in St. Peter's Square on Sunday, 24 April 1994:

> May prayer strengthen us for the spiritual battle we are told about in the Letter to the Ephesians: "Draw strength from the Lord and from His mighty power" (Ephesians 6:10). The Book of Revelation refers to this same battle, recalling before our eyes the image of St. Michael the Archangel (Revelation 12:7). Pope Leo XIII certainly had a very vivid recollection of this scene when, at the end of the last century, he introduced a special prayer to St. Michael throughout the Church. Although this prayer is no longer recited at the end of Mass, I ask everyone not to forget it and to recite it to obtain help in the battle against forces of darkness and against the spirit of this world.[61]

---

[61] "Prayer to St. Michael", June 25, 2010.
<http://www.ewtn.com/expert/answers/st_michael_prayer.htm>

Chapter 7
Fatima

The most significant event in salvation history since the days of the Apostles occurred at a place near Fatima, Portugal, in 1917. Three shepherd children claimed to see the Blessed Virgin Mary in a field called the Cova da Iria (Irene's Cove). The apparitions to the three children happened six times between 13 May and 13 October 1917.

Lucia dos Santos, ten years old, along with her first cousins Francisco, eight, and Jacinta Marto, seven, said the first apparition took place close to noon. The outline of the Fatima event was given at the outset by Blessed Mary at the first apparition when she said, *"Do not be afraid. I will not harm you. I come from Heaven. I have come to ask you to come here for six months, on the thirteenth day, at this same hour. Later I shall say who I am and what I desire. Will you offer yourselves to God and bear all the sufferings, which He sends you, in reparation for the sins which offend Him and in supplication for the conversion of sinners? Say the Rosary every day, to bring peace to the world and the end of the war."*

By 1917, the world was being torn apart by persecution, war and oppression. The horrific spectacle of World War I raged across much of Europe. The Tsar was being overthrown amidst turmoil and upheaval in Russia. In Portugal, seven years before the first visitation to the children of Fatima, revolutionists had seized power from King Manuel and declared Portugal a Republic. Three days after the proclamation of the Republic, all religious orders were suppressed. Churches were pillaged and monasteries and convents were attacked. The freemasons in charge of the Republic passed anti-clerical legislation, and all public celebration of religious feasts was suppressed and religious teaching was prohibited in all schools. The intent of those in power was to end the Catholic Church in Portugal within two generations. This was the state of the world in general, and Portugal in particular, at the time of Our Lady's apparition at Fatima.

For six months, Our Lady appeared to the three shepherd children, giving them a message for the world and promising a miracle so that all would believe in both the message and in God. The intricate workings of God in the apparitions are more apparent with the passing of time. While many details of the Fatima apparitions have been researched and documented, the two major elements are the message and the miracle. God intended the miracle to be witnessed by a multitude, hence it occurred during the sixth and final apparition. This allowed time for word of the events transpiring in the Cova to circulate throughout the region so a multitude could gather to witness it. The miracle took place during the final apparition both to underscore and to prove the message was from God. Given on 13 July 1917, at the half way mark of the apparitions, the message was given in three parts. The word secret is often used to describe it, because in the beginning the children did not reveal what Our Lady had told them. Over the years, according to the timeline of God, the message was revealed to the world. The first two parts became known in the middle years of the twentieth century but the third remained hidden, becoming infamous as 'the third secret of Fatima'. Throughout the latter half of the twentieth century many speculated about its contents. Some thought it told of a third world war, or a nuclear war, or the end of the world. But on 13 May 2000, all of the speculation ended, at least for a time, when Pope John Paul II finally revealed the third part of the message of Fatima to the world.

The first part of the message of Fatima consists of the vision of hell given by Blessed Mary to the three children:

As Our Lady spoke these last words, she opened her hands once more, as she had done during the two previous months. The rays of light seemed to penetrate the earth, and we saw as it were a sea of fire. Plunged in this fire were demons and souls in human form, like transparent burning embers, all blackened or burnished bronze, floating about in the conflagration, now raised into the air by the flames that issued from within themselves together with great clouds of smoke now falling back on every side like sparks in huge fires, without weight or equilibrium, amid shrieks and groans of pain and despair, which horrified us and made us tremble with fear. (It must have been this sight which caused me to cry out, as people say they heard me). The demons could be distinguished by their terrifying and repellent likeness to frightful and unknown animals, black and transparent like burning coals. Terrified and as if to plead for succor, we looked up at Our Lady, who said to us, so kindly and so sadly:

"You have seen hell where the souls of poor sinners go..."[62]

The second part of the message concerned conditional chastisements. These would occur if the requests of Blessed Mary were not done. On the other hand, if what she asked was done, many souls would be saved and there would be peace:

...To save them, God wishes to establish in the world devotion to my Immaculate Heart. If what I say to you is done, many souls will be saved and there will be peace. The war is going to end; but if people do not cease offending God, a worse one will break out during the pontificate of Pius XI. When you see a night illumined by an unknown light, know that this is the great sign given you by God that he is about to punish the world for its crimes, by means of war, famine, and persecutions of the Church and of the Holy Father.

To prevent this, I shall come to ask for the consecration of Russia to my Immaculate Heart, and the Communion of Reparation on the First Saturdays. If my requests are heeded, Russia will be converted, and there will be peace; if not, she will spread her errors throughout the world, causing wars and persecutions of the Church. The good will be martyred, the Holy Father will have much to suffer, various nations will be annihilated. In the end, my Immaculate Heart will triumph. The Holy Father will consecrate Russia to me, and she will be converted, and a period of peace will be granted to the world. In Portugal, the dogma of the Faith will always be preserved; etc...[63]

---

[62] Father Antonio Maria Martins, S.J., *Documents on Fatima & the Memoirs of Sister Lucia*. 2nd English ed. (Waite Park, MN: Park Press, 2002), 403. All rights reserved. Used with permission.
[63] Ibid., 404.

The third part of the message consisted of a vision that in essence repeated the first two parts of the message. The third part relates to the first two in the same metaphysical way a sheet of written music compares to how those notes sound when played. It is one thing to hear of tribulation, wars, a period of peace and the Triumph of the Immaculate Heart of Mary; it is quite another to see it. And see it they did:

> After the two parts which I have already explained, at the left of Our Lady and a little above, we saw an Angel with a flaming sword in his left hand; flashing, it gave out flames that looked as though they would set the world on fire; but they died out in contact with the splendor that Our Lady radiated towards him from her right hand: pointing to the earth with his right hand, the Angel cried out in a loud voice: 'Penance, Penance, Penance!'.

> And we saw in an immense light that is God: 'something similar to how people appear in a mirror when they pass in front of it' a Bishop dressed in White 'we had the impression that it was the Holy Father'. Other Bishops, Priests, men and women Religious going up a steep mountain, at the top of which there was a big Cross of rough-hewn trunks as of a cork-tree with the bark; before reaching there the Holy Father passed through a big city half in ruins and half trembling with halting step, afflicted with pain and sorrow, he prayed for the souls of the corpses he met on his way; having reached the top of the mountain, on his knees at the foot of the big Cross he was killed by a group of soldiers who fired bullets and arrows at him, and in the same way there died one after another the other Bishops, Priests, men and women Religious, and various lay people of different ranks and positions.

> Beneath the two arms of the Cross there were two Angels each with a crystal aspersorium in his hand, in which they gathered up the blood of the Martyrs and with it sprinkled the souls that were making their way to God. [64]

During the apparition of 13 July 1917, Blessed Mary promised a miracle so that all would believe: *"In October, I will tell you who I am and what I*

---

[64] Martins, *Documents on Fatima & the Memoirs of Sister Lucia*, 505.

want, and I will perform a miracle for all to see and believe."[65] The miracle on 13 October has become known as the Miracle of the Sun. It is the most public intervention of God in the history of man since the days of the Apostles. After her appearance to the three children that day, as Blessed Mary began her ascent, she pointed to the sun, and directed the rays emanating from her hands onto it. The sun began to swirl and spin, and all present could look at it for the duration of the miracle which by some accounts lasted ten minutes. As the sun twirled, it gave off various colors and the crowd was bathed in the colored light. Observers said "the sun danced." After a while, the sun dislodged itself from its moorings in the sky and descended towards the onlookers in a zigzag motion. Terrified, believing it to be the end of the world, the crowds screamed and shouted for mercy from God. Some said the sun appeared so close before it returned to its rightful place they felt they could touch its surface. All present were awed by the power of God. Additionally, witnesses reported that as the sun approached they could feel its heat. Before the sun descended it had been raining and the people's clothes were wet, but after the miracle everything was completely dry. Just as Blessed Mary had said, all present, including the atheists who had come to mock the crowds when no miracle occurred, believed.

After the miracle the children saw, in succession, what appeared to be vignettes of the three mysteries of the rosary. Lucia wrote later, "After Our Lady had disappeared into the immense distance of the firmament, we beheld St. Joseph with the Child Jesus and Our Lady robed in white with a blue mantle, beside the sun. St. Joseph and the Child Jesus appeared to bless the world, for they traced the Sign of the Cross with their hands. When, a little later, this apparition disappeared, I saw Our Lord and Our Lady; it seemed to me that it was Our Lady of Dolours. Our Lord appeared to bless the world in the same manner as St. Joseph had done. This apparition also vanished, and I saw Our Lady once more, this time resembling Our Lady of Carmel."[66]

Before the Miracle of the Sun, Our Lady said the famous remark often quoted when speaking of the Fatima apparitions: *"Do not offend the Lord our God any more, because He is already so much offended."*[67]

In the second part of the message, Blessed Mary said she would come to ask for the consecration of Russia to her Immaculate Heart and the Communion of Reparation on the First Saturdays.

---

[65] Ibid.,186.
[66] Ibid.,191.
[67] Ibid.,351,374.

Eight years after the Fatima events, when Sister Lucia was living in a convent in Pontevedra, Spain, Blessed Mary returned to ask for the Communion of Reparation on the First Saturdays. Sister Lucia wrote of the apparition of 10 December 1925, referring to herself in the third person:

> The Most Holy Virgin appeared to her [Sister Lucia], and by her side, elevated on a luminous cloud, was the child Jesus. The Most Holy Virgin rested her hand on her [Sister Lucy's] shoulder and as she did so, she showed her a heart encircled by thorns, which she was holding in her other hand. At the same time, the Child said:

> *Have compassion on the Heart of your Most Holy Mother, surrounded with thorns with which ungrateful men pierce it at every moment, and there is no one to make an act of reparation to remove them.*[68]

Then Our Lady said:

> *Look, my daughter at my heart surrounded by thorns with which ungrateful men pierce me at every moment by their blasphemies and ingratitude. You, at least, try to console me and announce in my name that I promise to assist at the moment of death, with all the graces necessary for salvation, all those who, on the first Saturday of five consecutive months shall confess, receive Holy Communion, recite five decades of the Rosary, and keep me company for fifteen minutes while meditating on the fifteen mysteries of the Rosary with the intention of making reparation to me.*[69]

Three and a half years later, on 13 June 1929, Blessed Mary came to ask for the consecration of Russia to her Immaculate Heart, as recorded in Volume I of *Fatima in Lucia's Own Words*:

> I had sought and obtained permission from my superiors and confessor to make a Holy Hour from eleven o'clock until midnight, every Thursday to Friday. Being alone one night, I knelt near the altar rails in the middle of the chapel and, prostrate, I prayed the prayers of the Angel. Feeling tired, I then stood up and continued to say the prayers with my arms in the form of a cross. The only light was that

---

[68] Martins, *Documents on Fatima & the Memoirs of Sister Lucia*, 279.
[69] Ibid.,279.

of the sanctuary lamp. Suddenly the whole chapel was illumined by a supernatural light, and above the altar appeared a cross of light, reaching to the ceiling. In a brighter light on the upper part of the cross, could be seen the face of a man and his body as far as the waist, upon his breast was a dove also of light and nailed to the cross was the body of another man. A little below the waist, I could see a chalice and a large host suspended in the air, on to which drops of blood were falling from the face of Jesus Crucified and from the wound in His side. These drops ran down on to the host and fell into the chalice. Beneath the right arm of the cross was Our Lady and in her hand was her Immaculate Heart. (It was Our Lady of Fatima, with her Immaculate Heart in her left hand, without sword or roses, but with a crown of thorns and flames). Under the left arm of the cross, large letters, as if of crystal clear water which ran down upon the altar, formed these words: "Grace and Mercy."

I understood that it was the Mystery of the Most Holy Trinity which was shown to me, and I received lights about this mystery which I am not permitted to reveal.

Our Lady then said to me: *"The moment has come when God asks the Holy Father, in union with all the Bishops of the world, to make the consecration of Russia to my Immaculate Heart, promising to save it by this means. There are so many souls whom the Justice of God condemns for sins committed against me, that I have come to ask for reparation: sacrifice yourself for this intention and pray."*

I gave an account of this to the confessor, who ordered me to write down what Our Lady wanted done.[70]

Two years and two months later, in August of 1931, at a chapel in Rianjo, Spain, Sister Lucia reported this important revelation to her bishop:

My confessor ordered me to inform Your Excellency about what happened a little while ago, between our Good God and myself: As I was asking God for the conversion of Russia, Spain and Portugal, it seemed that His Divine Majesty said to me:

---

[70] Martins, *Documents on Fatima & the Memoirs of Sister Lucia*, 393.

You console Me a great deal in asking Me for the conversion of those poor nations: Request it also of My Mother, while saying to Her often: Sweet Heart of Mary, be the salvation of Russia, Spain, Portugal, Europe and the whole world.

At other times say: By Thy Pure and Immaculate Conception, O Mary, obtain for me the conversion of Russia, Spain, Portugal, Europe and the whole world.

Make it known to My ministers, given that they follow the example of the King of France in delaying the execution of My command, they will follow him into misfortune. It is never too late to have recourse to Jesus and Mary.

In another text she wrote:

Later, through an intimate communication, Our Lord complained to me: *They did not wish to heed My request! ... Like the King of France they will repent of it, and they will do it, but it will be late. Russia will have already spread its errors throughout the world, provoking wars and persecutions against the Church. The Holy Father will have much to suffer.*[71]

In March of 1939, shortly before the outbreak of World War II, Lucia wrote:

Our Lord said to me once more: *"Ask, ask again for the promulgation of the Communion of Reparation of Mary on the First Saturdays. The time is coming when the rigor of My justice will punish the crimes of diverse nations. Some of them will be annihilated..."*[72]

The efforts on the part of the religious persons involved to better understand the requests from God form a part of Fatima's history. Upon conveying these requests, Sister Lucia was asked questions from the bishops, and, not always having an answer, at the first available opportunity she would ask Jesus or Blessed Mary through prayer. One such question dealt with the number of first Saturdays. On 29 May 1930, at a chapel in Tuy, Spain, Sister Lucia through prayer asked, "Why five Saturdays and not 9, or 7, in honor of the Sorrows of Our Lady?"

---

[71] Martins, *Documents on Fatima & the Memoirs of Sister Lucia*, 394.
[72] Ibid.

Through an interior locution from Jesus, Sister Lucia said she was given to understand that this related to the five main types of offences committed against the Immaculate Heart of Mary: blasphemies against the Immaculate Conception; against Mary's perpetual Virginity; against her Divine Maternity and the refusal to recognize her spiritual motherhood of mankind; for the offences of those who encourage in the hearts of children indifference, contempt and even hatred of their Immaculate Mother, and finally as reparation for those who outrage her in her holy images.[73]

According to Sister Lucia, Jesus further stated:

> *There, My daughter, is the reason why the Immaculate Heart of Mary inspired Me to request this small act of reparation, and in consideration of it, to move My mercy to forgive souls who have had the misfortune to offend Her. As for you, seek unceasingly, through your prayers and sacrifices, to move My mercy with regard to these poor souls.*

Questions were also asked about the form of the consecration of Russia to the Immaculate Heart of Mary. On 18 May 1936, Sister Lucia replied by letter to Father Jose Goncalves, her spiritual director:

> I have spoken with Our Lord about the subject, and not too long ago I asked Him why He would not convert Russia without the Holy Father making that consecration. Jesus answered, *'Because I want My whole Church to acknowledge that consecration as a triumph of the Immaculate Heart of Mary so that it may extend its cult later on and put the devotion to this Immaculate Heart beside the devotion to My Sacred Heart.'*[74]

The night "illumined by an unknown light" that would signal punishment from God in the form of war, famine, and persecution of the Church and the Holy Father occurred on 25 January 1938. The aurora was seen over the whole of Europe and as far south as southern Australia, Sicily, Portugal and across the Atlantic to Bermuda and southern California. All transatlantic radio communication was interrupted. Astronomers in New England said the lights differed from previous auroral displays in intensity, color, and direction of the beams. The immense arches of crimson light, with shifting areas of green and blue,

---

[73] Martins, *Documents on Fatima & the Memoirs of Sister Lucia*, 284.
[74] Ibid., 324.

radiated from a brilliant auroral crown near the zenith instead of appearing in the usual parallel lines.[75]

In 1952, Pope Pius XII consecrated the world and Russia to the Immaculate Heart of Mary, but his consecration was not done in union with the bishops, as originally requested, so it was "not accepted" by God. On 13 May 1946, Pius XII had the statue of Our Lady of Fatima found at the Shrine of Fatima crowned, proclaiming her "Queen of the World".[76] On 11 October 1954, Pius XII issued *Ad caeli Reginam*, his encyclical proclaiming the Queenship of Mary. Reigning during the crisis of World War II, in 1942 in the midst of that war, in the context of the message of Our Lady of Fatima, he consecrated the human race to the Immaculate Heart of Mary.

On 21 November 1964, Pope Paul VI renewed Pius XII's consecration to the Immaculate Heart of Mary privately, during Vatican II. On 13 May 1967, the fiftieth anniversary of the Fatima apparition, Paul VI became the first pope to visit the shrine.

On 13 May 1981, the feast day of Our Lady of Fatima, Pope John Paul II was shot in Saint Peter's Square. While recovering from his wounds, noting the date, he requested all the documents on Fatima. On 13 May 1982, at Fatima, he consecrated the world and Russia to the Immaculate Heart of Mary, but again this did not follow the request for the consecration. John Paul II had sent a notification to the bishops of the world, but it did not reach many of them in time. He also had the bullet removed during the surgery that saved his life placed in the crown of the statue of Our Lady of Fatima. John Paul publicly stated Blessed Mary intervened to save him, and he attributed this intervention to the prayers and sacrifices of the faithful, especially Jacinta, the Fatima visionary.

On 25 March 1984, the feast of the Annunciation to Blessed Mary, John Paul II made another consecration of the world and Russia to the Immaculate Heart of Mary in Saint Peter's Square. He had allowed ample time for his notification to reach the world's bishops, and later Sister Lucia told a papal nuncio God accepted the consecration.

The Fatima message specifically mentioned Russia as an instrument of persecution of Christians and of the broader world. After Russia became an atheistic communist state in 1917 and formed the USSR, it fomented unrest and wars in various places throughout the world to spread its atheistic doctrines. Our Lady referred to these in her Fatima message as

---

[75] Archive of the Most Severe Solar Storms, June 29, 2010. <www.solarstorms.org/SRefStorms.html>
[76] Martins, *Documents on Fatima & the Memoirs of Sister Lucia*, 12.

errors: *she [Russia]will spread her errors throughout the world, causing wars and persecutions of the Church. The good will be martyred, the Holy Father will have much to suffer, various nations will be annihilated.* Blessed Mary also prophetically said, "*The Holy Father will consecrate Russia to me, and she will be converted, and a period of peace will be granted to the world.*" After Sister Lucia confirmed God had accepted the consecration, the Vatican looked for changes in the world situation, and in particular for changes in the USSR. There are three reasons why the consecration can be said to be valid.

First, the only living Fatima visionary at the time of the consecration was Sister Lucia, and in 1989, she herself said it was valid:

"God accepted the consecration of March 25, 1984 as the one that fulfilled all the conditions for the conversion of Russia...The Pope was united to all the bishops in 1984. Those who did not want to be united with the Holy Father, the responsibility is theirs. The request for the Consecration was always an appeal to union. The Mystical Body of Christ (the Church) must be united! The members of the same Body are united!

His Excellency, the Bishop of Leiria, (Bishop Alberto Amaral) was here. He asked me and I told him, 'Yes. Now it was made.'

The Apostolic Nuncio (of Lisbon) [the representative of the Vatican] has been here recently and asked me, 'Is Russia now consecrated?' 'Yes. Now it is,' I answered. The Nuncio then said, 'Now we wait for the miracle.'

I answered, 'God will keep His word!'

As Editor of the Fatima Family Messenger I [Father Robert J. Fox] was told in 1989: "Lucia wants the message to get out to the world that the Collegial Consecration of Russia has taken place."

When Sister Lucia was told that not every Catholic bishop in the world joined in the 1984 consecration, Sister Lucia replied,

"It is true not every Catholic bishop responded to the Pope's request. That is their personal responsibility. But it was done right in 1984 and Our Lord has accepted the Collegial Consecration."

Sister Lucia has explained that an exact numerical number of 100% of the bishops was not required but the fact that most did join the Pope made for a moral totality.[77]

The second reason the consecration of 1984 is considered valid is because the Vatican said it was validly enacted.

The third reason is that history now shows it to be valid. The consecration was of Russia to Blessed Mary's Immaculate Heart, and a review of events related to the Russian Federation and its allies since March of 1984 reveals that it has been done. The major historical changes that took place in the USSR occurred over a number of years rather than days, and they are more apparent now when one looks back over the latter years of the twentieth century. Here is a list of events concerning the Soviet Union since the consecration of March 1984 as listed in a timeline found on EWTN's website[78], with additional entries:

Mar. 25, 1984   Pope John Paul II, united with all the bishops of the Church in a collegial bond, performs the consecration. Sister Lucia tells the papal nuncio to Portugal that the Consecration is fulfilled.

May 13, 1984   On the anniversary of Fatima, one of the largest crowds in Fatima history gathers at the shrine to pray the Rosary for peace.

May 13, 1984   On the anniversary of Fatima, an explosion at the Soviets' Severomorsk Naval Base destroys two-thirds of all the missiles stockpiled for the Soviets' Northern Fleet. The blast also destroys workshops needed to maintain the missiles as well as hundreds of scientists and technicians. Western military experts called it the worst naval disaster the Soviet Navy suffered since WWII.

Dec. 1984   The Soviet Defense Minister, mastermind of the invasion plans for Western Europe, suddenly and mysteriously dies.

---

[77] Martins, *Documents on Fatima & the Memoirs of Sister Lucia*, 42-43. All rights reserved. Used with permission. The editor of the *Fatima Family Messenger* at the time, referenced in the cited text, was Father Robert J. Fox.

[78] EWTN. Fatima Consecration. February 13, 2010.
<www.ewtn.com/expert/answers/FatimaConsecration.htm#pius11>

Mar. 10, 1985   Soviet Chairman Konstantin Chernenko dies.

Mar. 11, 1985   Soviet Chairman Mikhail Gorbachev elected.

Apr. 26, 1986   Chernobyl nuclear reactor accident occurs.

Dec. 8, 1987   Intermediate-Range Nuclear Forces Treaty (INF) to remove or reduce short-range nuclear missiles from Europe and elsewhere signed on the Feast of the Immaculate Conception.

May 12, 1988   An explosion wrecks the only factory that made the rocket motors for the Soviets' deadly SS 24 long-range missiles, which carry ten nuclear bombs each.

Aug. 29, 1989   Sr. Lucia affirms in correspondence that the consecration "has been accomplished" and that "God will keep His word."

Nov. 9, 1989   Fall of the Berlin Wall.

Nov-Dec 1989   Peaceful revolutions in Communist Czechoslovakia, Romania, Bulgaria, and Albania.

1990   East and West Germany are reunited.

Dec. 8, 1991   On the Feast of the Immaculate Conception of Mary, the presidents of Russia, Ukraine, and Belarus meet in Belovezh Forest in Belarus and declare the end of the Soviet Union, establishing the Commonwealth of Independent States in what becomes known as the Belavezha Accords.

Dec. 25, 1991   Dissolution of the Union of Soviet Socialist Republics, with the Soviet hammer and sickle flag being lowered from the Kremlin for the last time, fittingly on Christmas Day in the West.

Sister Lucia said a nuclear war would have erupted in 1985, had the Act of Consecration not been done. From the timeline, the USSR leaders planning the war died and their weapons of war were destroyed in the years immediately following the consecration.

Time magazine, writing a month or so after the Soviet naval disaster at Severomorsk, described its importance to the Soviet Navy:

Located near a cluster of naval installations on the Kola Peninsula, Severomorsk serves as a major ammunition depot for the 148 surface ships, nearly 200 submarines, 425 warplanes and one aircraft carrier that are attached to the Soviet Union's northern fleet. Normally, weapons would not have been stockpiled in such great quantities in one place. But in April the fleet had conducted the largest Soviet naval maneuvers ever in the North Atlantic; the missiles would have played a vital defensive role in the war games.[79]

The blast apparently caused such destruction that Western analysts initially thought a nuclear bomb had gone off. After studying satellite photos and other intelligence, they finally concluded that the "big bang" had come from the explosion of a large cache of conventional weapons.[80] Reports from other sources described a fire that started 13 May 1984 in Severomorsk and burned for five days, resulting in the explosion.[81]

After the consecration, the third part of the message of Fatima remained secret for many years. At Fatima on 13 May 2000, accompanied by Sister Lucia, Pope John Paul II beatified Jacinta and Francisco and at last the third part of the secret was revealed.

On 13 February 2005 Sister Lucia died. A couple of months later on 2 April 2005, John Paul also died, signaling to many the end of the Fatima events.

Pope Benedict XVI visited Fatima on 13 May 2010 to commemorate the tenth anniversary of the beatification of Jacinta and Francisco. Intriguingly, during his homily at Mass that day he said, "We would be mistaken to think that Fatima's prophetic mission is complete... May the seven years which separate us from the centenary of the apparitions hasten the fulfillment of the prophecy of the triumph of the Immaculate Heart of Mary, to the glory of the Most Holy Trinity."

---

[79] "Soviet Union: Big Bang." *Time*, 13 February 2010.
[80] Ibid.
[81] Russian Navy Blog: Soviet Naval Disaster of the Day. Severomorsk is Nearly Obliterated, 17 May 1984. February 13, 2010. <redbannernorthernfleet.blogspot.com/2008/05/soviet-naval-disaster-of-day.html>

One final thought on the Fatima apparitions has to do with blame for persecutions. Many have wondered why the Pope in union with the bishops did not fulfill Our Lady's request as soon as they learned of it, and so believe to this day that had they done so, much of the twentieth century horrors would have been averted. Recall that in her message, Blessed Mary said, *"If what I say to you is done, many souls will be saved and there will be peace... to prevent this [war, famine, and persecutions of the Church and of the Holy Father], I shall come to ask for the consecration of Russia to my Immaculate Heart, and the Communion of Reparation on the First Saturdays. If my requests are heeded, Russia will be converted, and there will be peace..."*

There are two requests, one directed at the Pope and the bishops, and the other directed at everyone:

> It is to be pointed out that the fault of the sufferings and persecutions of the twentieth century does not fall simply on bishops and the Holy Father. Because of insufficient prayer and penance in faith and love by members of the Church, the Pope was not able to accomplish the Consecration before 1984. The God of Justice required reparation for the outpouring of His Mercy. The faithful's acts of reparation, expressed especially by First Saturday acts of sacramental reparation, meditation and rosary prayers, would enable the Collegial Consecration of Russia to the Immaculate Heart of Mary to take place...In His mercy [God] revealed at Fatima what was needed to prevent the tragic events of the twentieth century.[82]

Summarizing:

- Jesus said that before the end (meaning the Short Time of Satan) the Gospel must first be preached to all nations as a witness. Earlier, we noted that by the start of the twentieth century, the gospel had been preached throughout the world. Now we have discovered that as the twentieth century approached, Pope Leo XIII was shown through a vision in 1884 that Satan chose the twentieth century to test the Church.
- In the first large scale public intervention from heaven since the days of the Apostles, Blessed Mary appeared at Fatima, Portugal in 1917 and warned in unprecedented detail of upcoming tribulations, providing remedies to avoid them.

---

[82] Martins, *Documents on Fatima & the Memoirs of Sister Lucia*, 511.

- Blessed Mary cited Russia and its errors as the main instrument that would be used (by Satan) to persecute the Church and the world. She cited upcoming wars and famines as a part of the world's punishments.
- Blessed Mary requested the Communion of Reparation on the First Saturdays, together with the consecration of Russia to the Immaculate Heart of Mary by the Pope in union with all of the bishops as the remedies that would prevent the coming persecutions.
- A great Miracle of the Sun occurred on 13 October 1917 to underscore the importance of the message of Fatima to the world. An estimated 70,000 people witnessed the event.
- Shortly after Blessed Mary's warnings, the communists overthrew the Tsar of Russia and an atheistic communist regime was installed in his place. Virtually overnight, the most populous Christian nation in the world became officially atheistic.
- As prophesied, wars, famines, and persecutions of the Holy Father took place throughout the middle years of the twentieth century as the communists spread errors of atheism—the rule of man without God—to half of the world's population, through force of arms. This reached its zenith on 13 May 1981, the feast of Our Lady of Fatima, when an assassination attempt originating from inside the Communist block was made on Pope John Paul II.
- On 25 March 1984, John Paul enacted the Consecration of Russia to the Immaculate Heart of Mary as requested by Blessed Mary.
- On 25 December 1991, the USSR (Communist Russia) was officially dissolved.
- On 13 May 2010, Pope Benedict XVI reminded us that the prophetic nature of Fatima is not over, and he prayed for the coming of the Triumph of the Immaculate Heart of Mary before the 2017 centenary of Fatima arrives.
- In hindsight, the events of the twentieth century were foretold at Fatima. Moreover, based on Pope Benedict's statement, the prophetic mission of Fatima is not yet complete.

The promised triumph of the Immaculate Heart of Mary has not yet occurred. There have been some foreshadowing events, however. One of these of course is the conversion of Russia from an atheistic state to a country where open religion is not only tolerated but also supported by the government. Recently the government allocated funds to repair and reconstruct some of the major churches damaged during the communist period. Russia is slowly moving from a period of darkness into the light. Another triumph of the Immaculate Heart of Mary was the survival of John Paul II after he was shot. The Fatima vision of 1917 showed the assassination of the "bishop dressed in white" but the Pope survived. The Pope attributed his survival to the intervention of Blessed Mary, due to many prayers and sacrifices, especially those of Fatima visionary Jacinta. Blessed Mary intervened to save Russia and she intervened to save John Paul II. These events serve as types for the complete fulfillment of the triumph of the Immaculate Heart of Mary promised by Our Lady.

There was one more important promise made at Fatima that has not yet been addressed. Recall that Blessed Mary said, *"The Holy Father will consecrate Russia to me, and she will be converted, and a period of peace will be granted to the world."* We have witnessed the beginnings of the changes in Russia. Additionally, God will grant a period of peace to the world.

Chapter 8
The Period of Peace

A valid consecration took place on 25 March 1984. Blessed Mary promised that God would grant a period of peace to the world once it had been enacted. To understand what this means a careful examination of events during and after that time is necessary. First, we see that the conversion of Russia took place shortly after the consecration, because official atheistic communism has collapsed and religious tolerance has increased throughout Russia. It follows that the period of peace also began when the consecration was completed, as promised. But many note since March 1984 there has been a steady stream of wars in diverse places, and this is certainly true. This presents two possibilities: As God's supreme emissary, Blessed Mary was wrong, or our understanding of what is meant by the period of peace is incorrect. The period of peace has begun, and yet there is war, so we can readily conclude that the period of peace does not mean the absence of war—the end of man fighting man. It might infer a lessoning of such conflicts, but not their complete eradication.

The Fatima event covers much of the twentieth century and continues even now, as we await the Triumph of the Immaculate Heart of Mary. To decode the phrase "period of peace" we need to look back at the past century, focusing on events related to Blessed Mary and peace.

The pontificate of Pope Benedict XV during World War I focused on peace efforts. During the war, Benedict placed the world under the protection of Blessed Mary. He added the last invocation *Mary Queen of Peace Pray for us* to the Litany of Loreto, a prayer asking for Blessed Mary's intercession, and he urged all Christians to ask Blessed Mary to obtain peace for the world. Eight days after this Blessed Mary appeared at Fatima as if in answer to the Pope's pleas, offering a remedy to bring peace.

After the war, towards the end of his papacy, Benedict focused his efforts on the emerging persecution of the Christians in the newly formed Russian-led federation, the Union of Soviet Socialist Republics, and the famine that appeared there after the chaos of the revolution. A Marian pope, Benedict advocated the mediatrix theology and in 1921 authorized the annual celebration of the Feast of Mary Mediator of all Graces in Belgium.

While she is known as Our Lady of Fatima, Blessed Mary actually appeared in a little place near Fatima called

> the Cova de Iria, a term derived from the Greek word "eirene," which means peace. Thus it can be affirmed, in a way, that Our Lady appeared in the Cova of Peace.[83]

There, Our Lady offered a remedy to bring peace when she said:

> *If what I say to you is done...there will be peace... I shall come to ask for the consecration of Russia to my Immaculate Heart, and the Communion of Reparation on the First Saturdays. If my requests are heeded...there will be peace...The Holy Father will consecrate Russia to me, and she will be converted, and a period of peace will be granted to the world...*

Close examination of the context in which Our Lady uses the word "peace" shows it is not our traditional use of the word, that is, the absence of war. Prior to mentioning the period of peace, Blessed Mary said *"if people do not stop offending God, another even worse war will begin..."* And she had already said that war can be punishment when she said, *"When you see*

---

[83] Martins, *Documents on Fatima & the Memoirs of Sister Lucia*, 133. All rights reserved. Used with permission.

a night illuminated by an unknown light, know that it is the great sign that God gives you that He is going to punish the world for its crimes by means of war, hunger, and persecutions of the Church and of the Holy Father." Blessed Mary warns of a time when God will punish man not only through war (man against man) but also by famine, Church persecutions, and persecutions and sufferings of the Pope. It is in this context that she speaks of the opposite of the punishments from God—a time when God will grant a period of "peace." Just as the punishment is not limited to war, the "peace" is not limited to "the absence of war." It is clear from the context that Blessed Mary means God will grant the world a period of reconciliation between God and man, once His representatives the Pope and the bishops invoke her through the Consecration of Russia to her Immaculate Heart, and Christians make the Communion of Reparation on the First Saturdays.

At Fatima Blessed Mary told us God is already too much offended and man must stop offending Him. Because of our sins, God needed to punish the world. However, if we honor Blessed Mary and through her request for us to convert we return to Him, because of His love for her God will reconcile with us. Blessed Mary calls this reconciliation the period of peace. It is a peace between man and God He gives us on her behalf. He does this to honor her and to teach us also to honor her.

It helps to remember that Blessed Mary is bringing a message from heaven and so she is speaking from the perspective of heaven, which is also the perspective of Scripture:

> *...because God wanted all fullness to be found in him and through him to reconcile all things to him, everything in heaven and everything on earth, by making peace through his death on the cross. You were once estranged and of hostile intent through your evil behavior; now he has reconciled you, by his death and in that mortal body, to bring you before himself holy, faultless and irreproachable—as long as you persevere and stand firm on the solid base of the faith, never letting yourselves drift away from the hope promised by the gospel...* [84]

While awaiting His return, we have not remained a faithful spouse. Rebellious mankind is, in a sense, at war with God; Mary makes it clear by what she says at Fatima about God already being offended too much that man has not persevered in the faith. But through the Consecration and Communion of Reparation once again the Almighty has extended an olive

---

[84] Catholic Online Bible-Col. 1,19-23, Mar 15, 2010. <http://www.catholic.org/bible/book.php?id=53>

branch, this time through His mother and our spiritual mother, granting us time to return to Him by once again following His Gospel truth, by converting. This is shown to us in the vision of the third part of the secret of Fatima, which ends with a vision of the period of peace where we see Blessed Mary restraining the fire of judgment while the souls make their way to God. It is important to note here that Blessed Mary is not acting against the will of God when she restrains the fire. The fire is restrained out of love—her love for us, and God's love for Our Lady and for us. It is in this vision that we see the fulfillment of Blessed Mary's role as our intercessor.

While Blessed Mary did not mean the period of peace would necessarily be a time of the absence of war, she did not preclude it either, so it has resulted in a lessening of tensions between the nations to some degree. Sadly, many who study the message of Fatima inexplicably forget its spiritual sense and confine it to a worldly perspective. Not finding peace among men, they conclude the consecration is yet to be made by a future pope and group of bishops. This distraction serves to undercut the importance of the roles of Fatima and Medjugorje in salvation history, because the apparitions of Medjugorje *are* the promised period of peace of Fatima.

Chapter 9
Medjugorje

Medjugorje, Bosnia-Herzegovina (in the former Yugoslavia), the site of an alleged apparition of Blessed Mary since 1981, has not been approved by the Catholic Church as worthy of belief, nor has it been ruled out as a supernatural occurrence. The Church's stance on Medjugorje is neutral, so to speak.

Since these apparitions have yet to be approved by the Church it is proper to refer to them as alleged apparitions, and so it is understood that the word alleged is implicit when speaking about them. The apparitions are ongoing and a special Vatican commission has been formed to investigate.

The apparitions began on 24 June 1981 when Our Lady appeared to several children on a hillside there. The next day, she appeared to Ivanka Ivankovic, age 15, Mirjana Dragicevic, age 16, Vicka Ivankovic (no relation), age 16, Ivan Dragicevic (no relation), age 16, Marija Pavlovic, age 16 and Jakov Colo, age 10. These six children have become known as the visionaries of Medjugorje, and 25 June is considered the anniversary date of the apparitions. Today, all of the visionaries are married with children of their own.

These visions are extraordinary for several reasons. First, they have continued on an almost daily basis. Second, some messages, particularly the earliest, speak directly to salvation history. Third, some of the 40 million pilgrims to Medjugorje report seeing various signs and wonders. Finally, the apparition is connected to the Fatima event.

The apparitions follow a distinct pattern. The Blessed Virgin appears at 6:40 each evening to each visionary. During the course of the daily apparitions, from time to time, Our Lady gives a visionary what is called a secret, a message that they are not permitted to reveal as of yet. Once a visionary has received ten secrets, that person's daily apparitions cease and from that point on the visionary receives a yearly apparition that will continue for the remainder of his or her life. To date, three of the six visionaries have received all ten secrets: Mirjana received her tenth secret on 25 December 1982, Ivanka received her final secret on 7 May 1985, and Jakov's daily apparitions ended on 12 September 1998. Mirjana receives her annual apparition on March 18, her birthday; Ivanka receives her yearly visit on June 25, the anniversary date of the apparitions; Jakov has an apparition of Blessed Mary each Christmas Day. In recent years, Mirjana has often had either a locution or an apparition on the second day of the month, during which she and Our Lady pray especially for unbelievers. Often a message is given. The other visionaries have nine secrets each

They repeatedly tell us the reason for the apparitions is the state of sin in the world at this time; the secrets are secondary. Blessed Mary has come to call the world to conversion, to a turning to God. The message is profoundly simple and recalls the Gospel: conversion to God through faith, prayer, fasting, reconciliation, and peace. Jesus came from heaven and taught us the Gospel. At Medjugorje, the Gospel is being repeated by another sent from heaven.

Some of the earliest messages, when combined with the framework of the secrets, speak directly to salvation history. The overall theme (for lack of a better word) of the apparition is the theme of Fatima: repent and turn to God and live in peace, or God, who is already too much offended, will punish. There is a difference though in the urgency of this message. If Fatima was the spring, Medjugorje is the autumn.

Some information about the secrets is known. As with Fatima, the secrets are not of a personal nature but instead pertain to world events. The first three have to do with warnings that implore conversion before it is too late. The first two might be catastrophic in nature to make people pause and reflect on the message given at Medjugorje. Visionary Mirjana hints at a regional catastrophe. Much of the third secret has been revealed: it is a sign. While it seems the first two secrets will bring fear, this sign will bring hope. It will show God's love and God's mercy. This sign will appear on the hill of the first apparition of Medjugorje, visible to all. It is intended for unbelievers as a last chance for conversion; believers do not need a sign. The visionaries say they know the date it will appear and they describe it as permanent, indestructible, and beautiful, something that has never before been on the earth, and those who do not believe in God will not be able to say it is of human origin. Our Lady said, *"You faithful must not wait for the sign before you convert; convert soon. This time is a time of grace for you. You can never thank God enough for His grace. The time is for deepening your faith, and for your conversion. When the sign comes, it will be too late for many."* [85]

The phrase "too late for many" has been the center of much fearful discussion. It has become clearer this message foretold the Medjugorje apparition would last many years. Our Lady said this in the early 1980s, and many hearing about Medjugorje then were already elderly. Blessed Mary knew many of the middle-aged and elderly who waited for the sign before converting would not live long enough to see it, so she lovingly and gently explained that everybody should convert, even before the sign appears.

The other seven secrets remain a mystery. Mirjana reported the majority of them are grave, catastrophic. Some of the seers cried after receiving the eighth, ninth, and tenth. As for dates, the seers say they will witness them. Blessed Mary has provided a mechanism to reveal each secret to the world. Mirjana was asked to choose a priest to aid in this, and she chose Father Petar Ljubici, then stationed at Medjugorje. Father Ljubici will serve as a witness: after seven days of fasting, he will reveal a secret three days before it occurs.

In addition to the framework of secrets, some of the messages focus on salvation history. Mirjana reported in 1982 that Blessed Mary told her:

> *Excuse me for this, but you must realize that Satan exists. One day he appeared before the throne of God and asked permission to submit the Church to a period of trial. God gave him permission to try the Church for one century. This century is under the power of the devil; but when the secrets confided to you come to pass, his power will be destroyed.* [86]

[85] "Overview of Medjugorje", June 25, 2010. <www.medjugorje.org/overview.htm>
[86] Ibid.

In another interview, Mirjana stated it as such: The Virgin Mary told her, "Satan has had immense power throughout the twentieth century."[87] The visionary was told that "a great cosmic battle is in full fury now for souls…the Eternal Father gave Satan one last challenge at His church, the twentieth century, and even some time preceding it and on into the Third Millennium."[88]

This echoes the vision of Pope Leo XIII. From Church teaching found in the catechism and based on Holy Scriptures, Satan's power is broken only at the very end of the last days of this present world.

Mirjana says that when Satan was granted the twentieth century to test the Church, there were three things he did not know:

— The Eternal Father would send Mary, the woman of His covenant with His people, throughout the century, to warn, encourage, and mother the souls struggling in this time of great darkness.

— The Eternal Father would permit such vast amounts of grace in the world as has never before been known in the history of mankind.

— The Eternal Father would send chosen souls who would remain faithful no matter what the allure or attack of Satan.[89]

Between 1984 and 1985, Blessed Mary said, *"The hour has come when the demon is authorized to act with all his force and power. The present hour, is the hour of Satan."*[90]

From 1982: *"These are my last apparitions to mankind. With the events which are preparing themselves, and which are near, the power which Satan still holds, will be withdrawn from him. The present century has been under his power."*[91]

Near the very beginning of the visitations, on 2 August 1981, Blessed Mary said, *"A great struggle is about to unfold, a struggle between my Son and Satan. Human souls are at stake."*[92]

---

[87] Janice T. Connell, *Visions of the Children*. Third ed. (New York: St. Martin's, 2007), 44.
[88] Ibid.
[89] Connell, *Visions of the Children*, 44.
[90] Rene Laurentin and R. Lejeune, *Messages and Teachings of Mary at Medjugorje*. (Milford, Ohio: The Riehle Foundation, 1988), 306.
[91] Ibid, 309.
[92] Rene Laurentin and R. Lejeune, *Messages and Teachings of Mary at Medjugorje*. (Milford, Ohio: The Riehle Foundation, 1988), 108.

On 4 April 1985, Our Lady said, *"I wish to keep on giving you messages as it has never been in history from the beginning of the world."*[93]

During an apparition at Medjugorje on 1 January 2001, Marija reported that "Our Lady gave a message: *'Tonight in a special way I desired you to be here. In a special way now when Satan is free from chains, I invite you to consecrate yourselves to my Heart and to the Heart of my Son.'*"

While saying nothing about any particular secret, visionary Ivanka says she knows ten secrets which involve the final chapters in the history of the planet earth.[94]

When the catastrophic secrets are combined with the messages, this apparition acquires an eschatological perspective. After 2000 years of visitations, Blessed Mary has come for the last time, announcing a special time of grace and conversion. She tells us to use this time well, and that it is urgent that we convert, now. Visionary Marija has said, "This is a time of great grace and mercy. Now is the time to listen to these messages and to change our lives. Those who do will never be able to thank God enough." Part III contains more messages from Blessed Mary at Medjugorje.

As with Fatima, as if to underscore the importance and authenticity of the apparitions, many visitors to Medjugorje report seeing what could only be called signs and wonders. And like the sun miracle at Fatima, many of these are luminous in nature. The apparitions at Fatima climaxed with the Miracle of the Sun. In contrast, many of the most striking luminous phenomena of Medjugorje occurred in the earliest days before it was widely known. Witnessed by most of the local villagers, they became the major reason why so many of them gathered at the apparitions. On 27 June 1981, a brilliant light witnessed by everyone and that illumined the entire area around the village preceded Our Lady's coming.[95] The next day the people gathered on Mount Podbrdo, the hill of the apparitions, saw the light that immediately preceded Our Lady's coming.[96] The sign observed on 2 August 1981, the Feast of Our Lady Queen of Angels, was like the dancing of the sun at Fatima.

One of the most important signs was the word MIR (Peace in Croatian), written on 24 August 1981 in large, fiery letters in the sky above the cross

---

[93] "Our Lady's Messages", June 25, 2010. <www.medjugorje.org/olmpage.htm>

[94] Janice T. Connell, *Visions of the Children*. Rev. and updated ed. (New York: St. Martin's Griffin, 2007), 84.

[95] Ana Yeseta, "Signs and Wonders in Medjugorje", June 27, 2010. <www.medjugorje.org/a_wonder.htm>

[96] Ibid.

on Mount Krizevac which overlooks the village. This particular sign was observed numerous times, with parish records reporting sightings on various days between 14 October 1981 and 3 October 1983.[97] Parish priest Father Jozo said that both he and the villagers were shocked into silence when they first saw the burning letters above the cross.

On 28 October 1981 several hundred people saw a fire that burned without consuming anything on the hill of the first apparition. That evening the Blessed Virgin told the seers: *It is a forerunner of the great sign.*[98]

Many other signs continue to be reported to the present day.

The final reason this apparition is extraordinary is its relationship to Fatima. Although separated by more than half a century, Medjugorje and Fatima are connected. Blessed Mary herself linked Medjugorje with Fatima when she said:

> *Dear Children! Today also I invite you to prayer, now as never before when my plan has begun to be realized. Satan is strong and wants to sweep away plans of peace and joy and make you think that my Son is not strong in his decisions. Therefore, I call all of you, dear children to pray and fast still more firmly. I invite you to self-renunciation for nine days so that, with your help, everything that I desire to realize through the secrets I began in Fatima, may be fulfilled.*
>
> *I call you, dear children, to now grasp the importance of my coming and the seriousness of the situation. I want to save all souls and present them to God. Therefore, let us pray that everything I have begun be fully realized. Thank you for having responded to my call."*[99]

Atheistic communism started in Russia within weeks of the Miracle of the Sun on 13 October 1917, but on the very day of this message, 25 August 1991, Russian President Boris Yeltsin signed a decree banning the Communist Party of the Soviet Union in Russia and nationalizing its property, effectively ending communism in that nation.

On 12 October 1981, Our Lady revealed her title for the apparition of Medjugorje: *I am the Queen of Peace.* On 26 June 1981, the second day, Blessed Mary said, "I desire to be with you in order to convert you and

---

[97] Rene Laurentin and R. Lejeune, *Messages and Teachings of Mary at Medjugorje.* (Milford, Ohio: The Riehle Foundation, 1988), 351.

[98] Ibid, 350.

[99] Our Lady of Medjugorje Message Page, retrieved March 8, 2010. <medjugorje.org/olmpage.htm>

reconcile the whole world." Father Rene Laurentin, an expert on Marian apparitions, explains this:

> God is the source of all reconciliation, the starting point, and the end of all unity...the word "reconciliation" alternates with the word "peace," with which it is identified. The word "peace" (in union with God) is the farewell of Our Lady at the end of the first apparition, Monday 25 June 1981.
>
> Go in the peace of God.
>
> The Virgin established... the bond between reconciliation and conversion...it is the essential finality of the message delivered to a divided world, because these divisions with God and among men lead to ruin.[100]

This explanation continues:

> After the wish for peace, which ended the apparition to the six seers on June 26th, the Virgin returns to it with insistence, in the private apparition to Marija...when she returned. She told Marija then:
>
> Peace, Peace, Peace! Be reconciled.
>
> The "conversion" asked by Our Lady is a return to God, with an understanding of... His loving will. That will is charitable for mankind and carries with it fruits of peace...we are invited to reconcile with others, beginning with our reconciliation with God.[101]

In other words, peace—union with God—as used by Our Lady in the context of the apparitions means reconciliation, first with God, and then with each other. From the Queen of Peace comes a message of peace, of reconciliation with God. We are called to turn back to God—to convert—so as to reconcile with Him. This connects Medjugorje to Fatima, because at Fatima Our Lady promised a period of peace once the Consecration was accomplished. As explained previously in the Period of Peace section, and here, by the word peace Our Lady means reconciliation with God. Medjugorje can be seen then as that period of peace promised at Fatima.

---

[100] Rene Laurentin and R. Lejeune, *Messages and Teachings of Mary at Medjugorje.* (Milford, Ohio: The Riehle Foundation, 1988), 39.

[101] Ibid, pp 39-41.

To His disciples Jesus said, *"my peace I give to you. Not as the world gives do I give it to you."*[102] He gave them peace in His divinity, a peace given by God to man. And at Medjugorje on 25 June 1987, Our Lady said, *"I want to invite you all to God's peace. I want each one of you to experience in your heart that peace which God gives."*

The luminous sign of the burning letters MIR (Croatian for "peace") above the cross on the mountain at Medjugorje during the earliest days of the apparition also confirm this. The angel in the third secret of Fatima pointed a flaming sword at the world, its flames blocked by Our Lady while souls make their way towards a cross and to God. The fiery letters above the cross remind us of this vision and once again ask us to choose peace, to choose to reconcile with God Who already reconciled with us by dying on the cross, over the flames of punishment.

The Miracle of the Sun, the hallmark of Fatima, has been seen by many visitors to Medjugorje over the years. This too serves as a sign to tell us the two apparitions are linked. Fatima and Medjugorje are two parts of one whole. Medjugorje is the fulfillment of the promise from Our Lady of Fatima of a period of peace.

---

[102] USCCB-NAB-John 14:27, March 17, 2010. <www.usccb.org/nab/bible/john/john14.htm>

PART II

The Reason For the Apparitions

The Church Age continues. We hold fast to the ketubah, the written Word left with us while our bridegroom resides with the Father. Over the last two thousand years, the Gospel has been preached throughout the world, meaning the groom's return is imminent. Heavenly events such as the appearance of the angel to Zechariah foretold the first coming and already we see events unfolding that might herald His return.

Apparitions of the twentieth century have a distinct eschatological tone. Just as the Holy Scriptures have a literal and a spiritual sense, so too do the apparitions. In Part II, the spiritual sense of Fatima and Medjugorje will be explored. And there are two other very important twentieth century apparitions with eschatological import that we haven't addressed yet, because their spiritual sense is much deeper than their literal details—the apparitions of Divine Mercy and Garabandal.

Chapter 10
Be Not Afraid

It cannot be emphasized enough how much we need to focus on Divine Mercy. It is a gift from Jesus specifically for the present time. The people of God have suffered a vicious battering from Satan during the last century. Many have become disheartened, broken, and fallen into grave sin, but through the gift of Divine Mercy we can obtain forgiveness of all sin and punishment for sin, and this is what is needed the most at this time.

In the messages from private revelations, as in the Bible, one common statement can always be found. God repeatedly tells us not to be afraid because He is peace and love and most importantly, mercy. It is important to remember this as we head into the years ahead. The phrase "the end of the world" leads to apprehension and if we knowingly ignore messages and warnings that Blessed Mary has given us over the past century, the phrase causes fear. Blessed Mary has been appearing throughout the twentieth century, asking us to turn back to God and reject our sinful ways.

Because of the apprehension and fear, now is the appropriate time to remember Divine Mercy. In the 1930s, Jesus appeared to a nun named Faustina (now a saint) to teach her and us about His mercy, which He said had been all but forgotten. He began His discourse to Saint Faustina by teaching some fundamental principles of God to help us understand a little better:

"On one occasion I was reflecting on the Holy Trinity, on the essence of God. I absolutely wanted to know and fathom who God is.... In an instant my spirit was caught up into what seemed to be the next world. I saw an inaccessible light, and in this light what appeared like three sources of light which I could not understand. And out of that light came words in the form of lightning which encircled heaven and earth. Not understanding anything, I was very sad. Suddenly, from this sea of inaccessible light came our dearly beloved Savior, unutterably beautiful with His shining Wounds. And from this light came a voice which said, *Who God is in His Essence, no one will fathom, neither the mind of Angels nor of man.* Jesus said to me, *Get to know God by contemplating His attributes.* A moment later, He traced the sign of the cross with His hand and vanished." (Diary, #30)[103]

Later, Saint Faustina was infused with knowledge of these attributes:

The first attribute which the Lord gave me to know is His holiness. His holiness is so great that all the Powers and Virtues tremble before Him. The pure spirits veil their faces and lose themselves in unending adoration, and with one single word they express the highest form of adoration; that is—Holy.... The holiness of God is poured out upon the Church of God and upon every living soul in it, but not in the same degree. There are souls who are completely penetrated by God, and there are those who are barely alive.

The second kind of knowledge which the Lord granted me concerns His justice. His justice is so great and penetrating that it reaches deep into the heart of things, and all things stand before Him in naked truth, and nothing can withstand Him.

The third attribute is love and mercy. And I understood that the greatest attribute is love and mercy. It unites the creature with the Creator. This immense love and abyss of mercy are made known in the Incarnation of the Word and in the Redemption [of humanity], and it is here that I saw this as the greatest of all God's attributes.(Diary, #180)[104]

---

[103] Faustina Maria Kowalska, *Diary of Saint Maria Faustina Kowalska: Divine Mercy in My Soul.* (Stockbridge, MA: Marian Press, 1987), 30. ©1987 Marian Fathers of the Immaculate Conception. All rights reserved. Used with permission.
[104] Ibid, 180.

And later Jesus told Saint Faustina:

> *Proclaim that mercy is the greatest attribute of God. All the works of My hands are crowned with mercy. (Diary, #301)*[105]

That was from a private revelation to Saint Faustina. Turning to Scripture, in James we find:

> *For the judgment is merciless to one who has not shown mercy; mercy triumphs over judgment.*[106]

Plainly speaking, if we fail to show mercy to others God will not show mercy to us on our Last Day. But, the mercy we show to others will triumph over our deserved judgment (our punishment). And we read this in the Beatitudes: *Blessed are the merciful, for they will be shown mercy.*[107]

Both the Bible and private revelation make it clear that God wants mercy from us and then He will grant it to us.

Returning to the private revelation of Saint Faustina, we read in her diary that Jesus told her repeatedly that He wanted His mercy better known in these times as a preparation for His final coming. Jesus appeared to Faustina in the 1930s and assured her the diary she was composing on His behalf and the Divine Mercy devotionals[108] would become widely known when the proper time arrived. He also showed her that she would one day be canonized. All of this came to pass in the year 2000, when Pope John Paul II instituted Divine Mercy Sunday and canonized Sister Faustina, which means the "proper time" to which Jesus referred is our time. Some of the messages He gave to Saint Faustina that illustrate this are:

> *You will prepare the world for My final coming. (Diary 429)*

> *Speak to the world about My mercy.... It is a sign for the end times. After it will come the Day of Justice. While there is still time, let them have recourse to the fountain of My mercy. (Diary, #848)*

---

[105] Ibid, 301.

[106] USCCB-NAB-James 2:13, June 3, 2010. <www.usccb.org/nab/bible/james/james2.htm >

[107] USCCB-NAB-Matthew 5:7

[108] Divine Mercy devotionals include the Chaplet of Divine Mercy, the Feast of Divine Mercy Sunday, and the image of Divine Mercy with the words "Jesus I Trust In You".

Tell souls about this great mercy of Mine, because the awful day, the day of My justice, is near. (Diary, # 965).

I am prolonging the time of mercy for the sake of sinners. But woe to them if they do not recognize this time of My visitation. (Diary, #1160)

Before the Day of Justice, I am sending the Day of Mercy. (Diary, #1588)

He who refuses to pass through the door of My mercy must pass through the door of My justice. (Diary, #1146).[109]

Jesus sends us the Day of Mercy before He comes again. The Feast of Divine Mercy Sunday, where both the sin and the punishment are forgiven in confession, was officially instituted after the year 2000 began. This is all according to God's plan, and indicates that the Day of the Lord, the last day, is near.

Jesus also reminded Faustina that we must show mercy, as it says in the Bible, and He was very specific about how we are to show mercy:

I demand from you deeds of mercy, which are to arise out of love for Me. You are to show mercy to your neighbors always and everywhere. You must not shrink from this or try to excuse or absolve yourself from it.

I am giving you three ways of exercising mercy toward your neighbor: the first—by deed, the second—by word, the third—by prayer. In these three degrees is contained the fullness of mercy, and it is an unquestionable proof of love for Me ... the first Sunday after Easter is the Feast of Mercy, but there must also be acts of mercy, and I demand the worship of My mercy through the solemn celebration of the Feast and through the veneration of the image which is painted. By means of this image I shall grant many graces to souls. It is to be a reminder of the demands of My mercy, because even the strongest faith is of no avail without works. (Diary, #742)[110]

As in His Gospels, here Jesus makes it clear that professions of our strong faith in God with our lips alone are useless. He demands works to demonstrate our love of God.

---

[109] Kowalksa, *Diary*. Used with permission.
[110] Ibid.

Jesus said the Pharisees loved Him with their lips alone. While they were rigorous in following the prayers and rituals of their religion, within a few centuries the rituals had lost their meaning and had become empty practices. They did not practice what they preached. So they were not able to recognize the Messiah when He stood in their midst. Worse, because of their rigor in following their rituals, they took on a "holier than thou" attitude.

It is not enough for us simply to go to church on Sunday and mouth familiar words. Nor is it enough to run to the church enthusiastically on Sunday morning and sing and pray at the top of our lungs with smiles on our faces, feeling joy in the Lord. Unless we show love to our neighbor with acts of kindness and mercy, we will hear Jesus say, "I do not know you."

Blessed Mary also speaks of not appearing before God upon our death with empty hands; they need to hold works of mercy—deeds, words, and prayers.

To those reading this who feel they haven't done enough (and who doesn't!), there is still time to fill our hands with deeds of mercy. We can pray for our neighbors and speak kindly to and of others. And we can always offer a helping hand—we can volunteer or donate our time. Remember that it is never too late to start. So we must not be afraid. We have a little time yet. We must trust in His mercy and act accordingly, and then His Mercy is ours!

But time is short, so we should begin as soon as possible. This is why Blessed Mary says in her apparitions that it is urgent we turn back to God now. Prayers for others are an act of mercy, and this is one reason why she asks us to pray for our neighbors and the souls in purgatory, and this is why she asks us to fast—to show our love for God and neighbor. She reminds us always to show kindness to our neighbors in word and deed, at the office, in the parking lot, in our own backyard.

Blessed Mary is telling us how to fill our hands with mercy.

The visionaries of Medjugorje tell us, "Those who listen to Blessed Mary and convert will never be able to thank God enough." Sister Lucia, the Fatima seer, said as long as we are alive, it is never too late to turn back to God and repent, and to show Him the love we have for Him.

Jesus told Saint Faustina that He wants us to trust in His Mercy. As she wrote in her diary:

The mercy of God, hidden in the Blessed Sacrament, the voice of the Lord who speaks to us from the throne of mercy: *Come to Me, all of you.*

[A part of the] Conversation of the Merciful God with a Sinful Soul.

Soul: Lord, I doubt that You will pardon my numerous sins; my misery fills me with fright.

Jesus: *My mercy is greater than your sins and those of the entire world. Who can measure the extent of my goodness? For you I descended from heaven to earth; for you I allowed myself to be nailed to the cross; for you I let my Sacred Heart be pierced with a lance, thus opening wide the source of mercy for you. Come, then, with trust to draw graces from this fountain. I never reject a contrite heart. Your misery has disappeared in the depths of My mercy. Do not argue with Me about your wretchedness. You will give me pleasure if you hand over to me all your troubles and griefs. I shall heap upon you the treasures of My grace. (Diary, #1485)*[111]

At another place she writes these words of Jesus:

I perform works of mercy in every soul. The greater the sinner, the greater the right he has to My mercy. My mercy is confirmed in every work of My hands. He who trusts in My mercy will not perish, for all his affairs are Mine, and his enemies will be shattered at the base of My footstool.(Diary, #723)[112]

And one more of so many passages found in her diary that tell us how much Jesus wants us to trust in Him:

[Jesus said to Saint Faustina:]...encourage the souls with whom you come in contact to trust in My infinite mercy. Oh, how I love those souls who have complete confidence in Me. I will do everything for them. (Diary, #294)[113]

These messages about the trust we need to have in Jesus come from the private revelations to Saint Faustina in the 1930s. Repeatedly Jesus told her

---

[111] Kowalska, *Diary.* Used with permission.
[112] Ibid.
[113] Ibid.

He was appearing to her so that the world would be reminded of His mercy as a preparation for His final coming.

In Sacred Scripture we also find God speaking of trust in His name before His final coming. In prophecies of the last days in the Book of Malachi it says:

> *And a record book was written before him of those who fear the LORD and trust in his name. And they shall be mine, says the LORD of hosts, my own special possession, on the day I take action. And I will have compassion on them, as a man has compassion on his son who serves him.*[114]

It says *"trust in his name"*, and become His special possession on the Last Day. His name is Jesus. On the Divine Mercy image revealed to St. Faustina it says, *"Jesus I trust in You."*

We must not be afraid! We must perform works of mercy. And most of all, we must trust in Jesus' mercy. As we head toward the Last Day of either our lives or this present age:

Be Not Afraid!

Chapter 11
The End

We need to address the biblical meaning of the phrase "end of the world" before explaining the twentieth century's apparitions. Depictions in the media distort its biblical meaning. From Scripture, it is clear the world never ends. The Last Day found in Scripture is the last day of this present world, which is remade at that time into its original, perfect state.

From the *Catechism of the Catholic Church*:

> At the end of time, the Kingdom of God will come in its fullness. After the universal judgment, the righteous will reign forever with Christ, glorified in body and soul. The universe itself will be renewed.

> Sacred Scripture calls this mysterious renewal, which will transform humanity and the world, "new heavens and a new earth."

> In this new universe, the heavenly Jerusalem, God will have his dwelling among men.

> Those who are united with Christ will form the community of the redeemed, "the holy city" of God, "the Bride, the wife of the Lamb."

> The visible universe, then, is itself destined to be transformed, "so that the world itself, restored to its original state, facing no further

obstacles, should be at the service of the just," sharing their glorification in the risen Jesus Christ.[115]

The end of the world is called the Last Day, the Terrible Day of the Lord, and the Day of Wrath, among others. God once destroyed the earth with water; the Bible tells us the next time it will be with fire.

...the coming of the day of God, because of which the heavens will be dissolved in flames and the elements melted by fire.[116]

On the last day all will find themselves surrounded by fire. The fire will be a fire of purification for those in a state of grace, and of hell for those who are not. The unrepentant unrighteous will be burned to ashes; that is they will be consumed by the fire. The repentant will pass through an intense, compressed form of purgatory, and then come out of the fire cleansed and sanctified for heaven.

In all the land, says the LORD, two thirds of them shall be cut off and perish, and one third shall be left. I will bring the one third through fire, and I will refine them as silver is refined, and I will test them as gold is tested.[117]

The work of each will come to light, for the Day will disclose it. It will be revealed with fire, and the fire (itself) will test the quality of each one's work. If the work stands that someone built upon the foundation, that person will receive a wage. But if someone's work is burned up, that one will suffer loss; the person will be saved, but only as through fire.[118]

A footnote explains the meaning of *the Day*: the great day of Yahweh, the day of judgment, which can be a time of either gloom or joy. Fire both destroys and purifies.[119]

Of that day, the humble, soft-spoken Blessed Mary told Saint Faustina, in the 1930s:

You have to speak to the world about His great mercy and prepare the world for the Second Coming of Him who will come, not as a merciful Savior, but

---

[115] *Catechism* 1042-1045,1047.
[116] USCCB-NAB-2 Peter 3:12, March 15, 2010. <www.usccb.org/nab/bible/2peter/2peter3.htm>
[117] USCCB-NAB-Zechariah 13:8-9
[118] USCCB-NAB-1 Corinthians 3:13-15
[119] USCCB-NAB-1 Corinthians 3, Footnote 7

as a just Judge. Oh how terrible is that day! Determined is the day of justice, the day of divine wrath. The angels tremble before it. Speak to souls about this great mercy while it is still the time for granting mercy.(Diary, #635)[120]

And at Medjugorje, Blessed Mary said:

The only thing that I would want to tell you is to be converted. Make that known to all my children as quickly as possible. No pain, no suffering is too great for me in order to save the world; but I plead with you, be converted. You cannot imagine what the Eternal Father will send to earth. That is why you must be converted! Renounce everything. Do penance. Express my thanks to all my children who have prayed and fasted. I carry all this to my Divine Son in order to obtain an alleviation of His justice against the sins of mankind. I thank the people who have prayed and fasted. Persevere and help me to convert the world.

Jesus said, *"I Am the Resurrection."*[121] The phrase encompasses much more than Jesus' rising from the dead, if that were possible. When man sinned, the entire cosmos became disordered, but Jesus will restore everything to the state of its creation before the Serpent's temptation of Adam and Eve. In the Book of Revelation Jesus says to us, *"Behold I make all things new."*[122] Our creed teaches the resurrection of the dead. Why have a physical body if we live in a spiritual place? We will live on the renewed earth. The earth will be perfect and an extension of what we now call heaven. Jesus prayed, *"your will be done on earth as it is in heaven."*[123]

On the Last Day everything will be made perfect again, through a transforming fire. In the Book of Daniel, we find a type for what will happen on the Last Day:

A herald cried out: "Nations and peoples of every language, when you hear the sound of the trumpet ... you are ordered to fall down and worship the golden statue which King Nebuchadnezzar has set up. Whoever does not fall down and worship shall be instantly cast into a white-hot furnace."[124]

Compare this passage to what we are told of Jesus the King when He comes on the Last Day: the nations of the earth will hear the sound of the

---

[120] Kowalska, *Diary*. All rights reserved. Used with permission.
[121] USCCB-NAB-John 11:25, May 31, 2010. <www.usccb.org/nab/bible/john/john11.htm>
[122] USCCB-NAB-Revelation 21:5
[123] USCCB-NAB-Matthew 6:10
[124] USCCB-NAB-Daniel 3:4-6, March 15, 2010. <www.usccb.org/nab/bible/daniel/daniel3.htm>

trumpet, and fall down and worship Him as He comes in glory. This reveals the passage in Daniel to be a type for that Day.

The story tells how the Israelites Shadrach, Meshach, and Abednego refused to worship the false god of Babylon and were cast into a furnace, but lived. On the Last Day, we will be thrown into the furnace, the fire of Truth, and those who have faith in God, love Him and do His will and seek His mercy, will be saved:

> *Shadrach, Meshach, and Abednego answered King Nebuchadnezzar, "There is no need for us to defend ourselves before you in this matter. If our God, whom we serve, can save us from the white-hot furnace and from your hands, O king, may he save us!" They were bound and cast into the white-hot furnace with their coats, hats, shoes and other garments.*

This prefigures how we will find ourselves in the fire of the Last Day, just as we are, with our clothes, shoes, and other garments.

> *They walked about in the flames, singing to God and blessing the Lord.*
> *"Bless the Lord; praise and exalt him above all forever. For he has delivered us from the nether world, and saved us from the power of death; He has freed us from the raging flame and delivered us from the fire...his mercy endures forever."*

> *Hearing them sing, and astonished at seeing them alive, King Nebuchadnezzar...asked... "Did we not cast three men bound into the fire?" "Assuredly, O king," they answered....*

> *"I see four men unfettered and unhurt, walking in the fire, and the fourth looks like a son of God."*
> *Then Nebuchadnezzar came to the opening of the white-hot furnace and called to Shadrach, Meshach, and Abednego: "Servants of the most high God, come out." Thereupon Shadrach, Meshach, and Abednego came out of the fire...they saw that the fire had had no power over the bodies of these men; not a hair of their heads had been singed, nor were their garments altered; there was not even a smell of fire about them.*[125]

On the last day, the faithful standing amidst the white-hot flames will hear, "Servants of the most high God, come out." And those in Purgatory

---

[125] USCCB-Daniel 3:16-18,21,24,88,9-94

on the last day will hear it, too. A type for this is found in the New Testament when Jesus commanded Lazarus:

> *Jesus told her, "I am the resurrection and the life; whoever believes in me, even if he dies, will live… And when he had said this, he cried out in a loud voice, "Lazarus, come out!"* [126]

The fire that descends on the last day will come from the Holy Spirit. Before He ascended to Heaven, Jesus told the disciples the Holy Spirit would be sent to spiritually perfect them: *"[The Advocate] will guide you to all truth."* [127]

The events of the first Pentecost serve as a type for what will happen at the end. At Pentecost, the Holy Spirit descended upon the Church, which consisted of the Apostles, Blessed Mary, and the disciples gathered in the Upper Room in Jerusalem:

> *And when the days of the Pentecost were accomplished, they were all together in one place: And suddenly there came a sound from heaven, as of a mighty wind coming, and it filled the whole house where they were sitting. And there appeared to them parted tongues as it were of fire, and it sat upon every one of them: And they were all filled with the Holy [Spirit]…* [128]

Here we see a physical manifestation of the presence of the Holy Spirit, as a fire above each one in the Upper Room as he or she is purified and filled with all Truth. Jesus said about the coming of the Holy Spirit:

> *Whoever loves me will keep my word, and my Father will love him, and we will come to him and make our dwelling with him. Whoever does not love me does not keep my words… If you keep my commandments, you will remain in my love… If I had not come and spoken to them, they would have no sin; but as it is they have no excuse for their sin. Whoever hates me also hates my Father.* [129]

This says much for all times but especially for our time. Jesus speaks of love and hate, and defines them by action. Those who keep His commandments love Him and He loves them. *If I had not come and spoken*

---

[126] USCCB-NAB-John 11:25,43 March 15, 2010. <www.usccb.org/nab/bible/john/john11.htm>

[127] USCCB-NAB-John 16:13

[128] Douay-Rheims Catholic Bible– Acts 2:1-4, Mar. 15, 2010. <www.drbo.org/chapter/ 51002.htm>

[129] USCCB-NAB-John 14:23-26, 15:9-10,22-23

to them, they would have no sin, but as it is they have no excuse for their sin. Jesus spoke to those of His time directly, and later He speaks to us through the Gospel message taught by His Church, guided by the Holy Spirit. After Jesus finished speaking truth to the people of God and returned to His Father, the Holy Spirit descended. And now, Blessed Mary has come on behalf of her Son to speak to us once again in truth. After this grace, when her time to speak to us is completed, the Holy Spirit will again descend as fire *"and when he comes he will convict the world in regard to sin and righteousness and condemnation"*.[130] This means the Holy Spirit's role will be prosecutorial.

Because the Truth has been spoken to the world through the Church, the Holy Spirit can convict the world based on how people responded. All those alive at the end will be convicted and handed over to the Son for final judgment of the living and the dead, who also arise. All of our self-centered works will have been consumed in the fire of conviction, but love and mercy we showed others will remain as we go before our Judge. Upon sentencing, Jesus will take into account our deeds of love and mercy.

Believers and non-believers alike will know the Truth on that day, just as the disciples were filled with Truth on the first Pentecost Sunday when the Holy Spirit descended upon them. This will cause "wailing and grinding of teeth" amongst the unbelievers and the hypocrites, those who say they believe with their lips but perform evil deeds, as they acknowledge the truth of the Gospel and are condemned. But just as it burned through the disciples and refined them into children of God, at the end the righteous alive at that time will be purified by the consuming fire of God; they will die to self and come out of the fiery furnace foretold in Daniel *and shine like the sun in the kingdom of their Father.*[131] In Matthew 13:38-42 Jesus tells the parable of the weeds in the field:

> *The good seed [is] the children of the kingdom. The weeds are the children of the evil one, and the enemy who sows them is the devil. The harvest is the end of the age.... Just as weeds are collected and burned (up) with fire, so will it be at the end of the age.*
> *The Son of Man will send his angels, and they will collect out of his kingdom all who cause others to sin and all evildoers. They will throw them into the fiery furnace, where there will be wailing and grinding of teeth.*

---

[130] USCCB-NAB-John 16:8-11
[131] USCCB-NAB-Matthew 13:41-43, 24:51, March 15, 2010.
<www.usccb.org/nab/bible/matthew/matthew13.htm>

Fire coming on the Last Day is also found in the Book of Malachi, where again we see the faithful servants of God come out of the fire and live:

> *And you shall return, and shall see the difference between the just and the wicked: and between him that serveth God, and him that serveth him not.* [132] *For behold the day shall come kindled as a furnace: and all the proud, and all that do wickedly shall be stubble: and the day that cometh shall set them on fire, saith the Lord of hosts, it shall not leave them root, nor branch.* [133]

At Medjugorje, Blessed Mary said something similar to Matthew's parable of the weeds to Mirjana on 15 August 1985:

> *My angel, pray for the unbelievers. People will tear their hair, brothers will plead with brothers, they will curse their past godless lives lived without God. They will repent but it will be too late. Now is the time for conversion. I have been exhorting you for the past four years. Pray for them. Invite everyone to pray the rosary.* [134]

About the descent of the Holy Spirit that is to come, it is interesting to note what St. Paul writes:

> *The earthly man is the pattern for earthly people, the heavenly man for heavenly ones. And as we have borne the likeness of the earthly man, so we shall bear the likeness of the heavenly one. What I am saying, brothers, is that mere human nature cannot inherit the kingdom of God: what is perishable cannot inherit what is imperishable. Now I am going to tell you a mystery: we are not all going to fall asleep, but we are all going to be changed, instantly, in the twinkling of an eye, when the last trumpet sounds. The trumpet is going to sound, and then the dead will be raised imperishable, and we shall be changed, because this perishable nature of ours must put on imperishability, this mortal nature must put on immortality.* [135]

The dead will rise and receive transfigured bodies meant for living in Heaven, the Kingdom of God. But the living too are changed in an instant,

---

[132] Douay-Rheims Catholic Bible– Mal. .3:18, Mar. 15, 2010. <www.drbo.org/chapter/44003.htm>

[133] Douay-Rheims Catholic Bible– Mal.. 4:1, Mar. 15, 2010. <www.drbo.org/chapter/44004.htm>

[134] Wayne Weible, *The Final Harvest* Revised and Updated. (CMJ Marian Publishers, 2002), 84.

[135] Catholic Online Bible-1 Cor. 15:48-53, Mar 15, 2010.
<http://www.catholic.org/bible/book.php?id=53>

purified and transfigured into their incorruptible bodies meant for living in the Heaven now on earth, on the Last Day. This change will be similar but more complete than what the disciples experienced during Pentecost, because the descent of the fiery Holy Spirit on Pentecost is a type for the last day.

Peter also speaks of the fire that is to renew the earth:

> Knowing this first, that in the last days there shall come deceitful scoffers, walking after their own lusts, Saying: Where is his promise or his coming? for since the time that the fathers slept, all things continue as they were from the beginning of the creation.
> For this they are willfully ignorant of, that the heavens were before, and the earth out of water, and through water, consisting by the word of God. Whereby the world that then was, being overflowed with water, perished.
> But the heavens and the earth which are now, by the same word are kept in store, reserved unto fire against the day of judgment and perdition of the ungodly men...the day of the Lord shall come as a thief, in which the heavens shall pass away with great violence, and the elements shall be melted with heat, and the earth and the works which are in it, shall be burnt up. Seeing then that all these things are to be dissolved, what manner of people ought you to be in holy conversation and godliness? Looking for and hasting unto the coming of the day of the Lord, by which the heavens being on fire shall be dissolved, and the elements shall melt with the burning heat? But we look for new heavens and a new earth according to his promises, in which justice dwelleth.[136]

Here we are reminded of the flood and told of the fire that is to come. And in 1 Peter we are read:

> God patiently waited in the days of Noah during the building of the ark, in which a few persons, eight in all, were saved through water. This prefigured baptism, which saves you now.[137]

And God patiently waits in our day, while the Ark, Mary, the herald of righteousness, calls us to return to God. Noah's ark carried the righteous through water that purified and renewed the earth. Is the Ark Blessed

---

[136] Douay-Rheims Catholic Bible–2 Peter 3:3-13, Mar. 15, 2010. <www.drbo.org/chapter/ 68003.htm>
[137] USCCB-NAB-1 Peter 3:20-21

Mary here to turn us back to righteousness and save us through the fire that will purify and renew the world a second time?

Jesus spoke of baptism when He said to Nicodemus, *"Amen, amen, I say to you, no one can enter the kingdom of God without being born of water and Spirit."*[138]

And John the Baptist said, *"I am baptizing you with water, for repentance, but the one who is coming after me is mightier than I...He will baptize you with the holy Spirit and fire."*[139]

There is baptism of water and baptism of the Holy Spirit and fire; the world was cleansed the first time by water and will be purified the second time by the Holy Spirit and fire.

> *In the beginning God created heaven, and earth. And the earth was void and empty, and darkness was upon the face of the deep; and the spirit of God moved over the waters.*[140]

The Holy Spirit formed the world in the beginning. The fiery Holy Spirit will re-form the world at the end into a new heaven and a new earth. The earth will become a new Garden of Eden, and we will be reunited with our loved ones and live as the family of God, Who will dwell with His people forever.

Fatima's Miracle of the Sun was a foreshadowing of a new Pentecost, a sign of the future outpouring of the Holy Spirit. Is it connected to the triumph of the Immaculate Heart of Mary?

---

[138] USCCB-NAB-John 3:5
[139] USCCB-NAB-Matthew 3:11
[140] Douay-Rheims Catholic Bible – Book of Genesis 1:1-2, April 30, 2010.
<www.drbo.org/chapter/01001.htm>

Chapter 12
The Meaning of Fatima

At Fatima, Blessed Mary foretold the most important historical events of the twentieth century. The rise of atheistic communism in Russia, World War II, famines, wars, the assassination attempt on the Pope, apostasy, and the period of peace were foretold in 1917, and all of it happened. But more was announced and promised. Through the Fatima apparition, God gives us important revelations about salvation history. By studying the apparition from that viewpoint, using the spiritual senses of Scriptures and especially the typological sense as a lens, we can discover the reason for Fatima, and what it announces to the world.

On the simplest level we notice the Fatima message is one message given in three parts, which interestingly enough follows the pattern of the timeline we discovered in Sacred Scripture—an end times period broken into three sub-periods. In the first part of the Fatima message, Blessed Mary opens her hands, which open the ground, and the children peer into the cavern of hell. Revelation chapter 20 speaks of the abyss of hell being opened and Satan unleashed for a short time, and the children of Fatima are shown hell opened up. The second part of the message focuses on great persecutions, including a catastrophic second world war, other wars, famine, martyrdom, sufferings of the Church and the Holy Father, and the annihilation of nations. Lastly, the third part of the message of Fatima climaxes with the period of peace/reconciliation in which Blessed Mary is shown interceding as souls make their way to God. (From our earlier discussion, the period of peace is a period of reconciliation between man and God.) A comparison of the three parts of the Fatima message with our end times timeline looks like this:

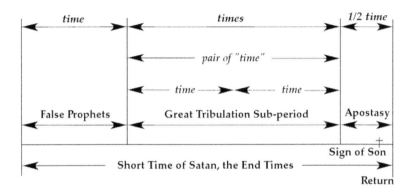

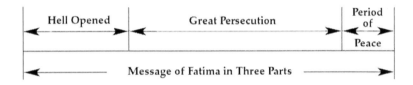

While the duration of each part of the message spoken at Fatima is not fully known, I have taken the liberty here to proportion them the same as on the end times timeline. Blessed Mary did say the period of reconciliation would begin when the Pope consecrated Russia to her Immaculate Heart, and we know that happened on 25 March 1984. We also know the second part of the message happened from the time of Fatima until the time of the consecration. As with the end times timeline, graphically the beginning and ending of the parts of the message seem very sharply defined, but in actuality they flow together seamlessly. Church sufferings, for example, did not immediately cease on 25 March 1984, nor did Russian atheism and communism. It is unrealistic to expect God to act in such a pretentious manner, in a way that inhibits the freedom of the human will. It would be "expecting too much".

The Thirteenth of the Month is the Day of Deliverance of the People of God

On another level, anyone who studies the apparition of Fatima quickly notices its association with the number thirteen.

First, the apparitions occurred on the thirteenth of the month for a total of six months. Then, on 13 June 1929, the Holy Trinity and Blessed Mary appeared to Sr. Lucia and made the request for the Act of Consecration. Pope John Paul II was shot on 13 May 1981, as prophesied in the third part of the secret of Fatima. The apparition was approved on 13 October 1930, thirteen years to the day of the last apparition. Lastly, Sister Lucia died on 13 February 2005.

The use of the number thirteen was willed by God; it is not a coincidence. The simplest explanation is that the number thirteen represents one God in three Persons. However, it goes much deeper.

Esther is a type for Blessed Mary. In the Book of Esther, the thirteenth of the month of Adar is mentioned six times, and at Fatima Blessed Mary appeared on the thirteenth of the month six times.

In the Book of Esther, Haman, the Persian King's minister and the second most important person in the kingdom, persuaded the king to kill every Jew in the kingdom in what would be the first Holocaust. Following that, Haman cast lots (purim) to determine the day of annihilation, and the result was the thirteenth of Adar. But Haman's plans to eradicate the Jews residing in Persia were foiled by Esther, King Ahasuerus's queen. Unbeknown to the king, Queen Esther was Jewish. Esther intervened to save her people who instead of being exterminated on the thirteenth, were delivered from annihilation. Jews commemorate this with the yearly feast of Purim. This is the most plausible explanation for Queen Mary, who is Jewish, to appear on the thirteenth of the month six times, and through Fatima events to underscore the number thirteen.

Interestingly, the Book of Ester is the only book in the Bible that does not mention God (it hints at God, but does not directly mention Him). This can be taken to mean that God many times acts in ways that are not readily apparent; that it is His work done through someone else. All that Blessed Mary is doing and has done in her apparitions, especially her apparitions in the twentieth century, are the will of God being carried out through her.

Many great Catholic saints and mystics throughout the ages have prophesied that the glory of Blessed Mary will be made known as she herself will lead and help deliver her offspring from the snares of Satan in the end times, just as Queen Esther did.

The typology of Esther is clear. The Book of Esther reflects a situation in which Jews were an ethnic-religious minority—scattered in many countries throughout the empire, organized in self-contained, self-governing communities and subjected to intensive and sometimes violent hatred by some members of the surrounding society. The Jews in the story are symbolic of the people of God in today's world, symbolized by the Persian Empire. The Jewish Queen Ester is symbolic of Blessed Mary. The thirteenth as the day chosen by lots is indicative of the thirteenth of October, 1917, and the promise of the triumph of Mary's heart over us and over evil, thus delivering her offspring from the evil one. The day of annihilation, the thirteenth of the month, became the day of triumph for the Jews over their enemies. At Fatima, appearing on the thirteenth of the month, Blessed Mary promises us that in the end her Immaculate Heart will triumph. The words "in the end" point to a future final triumph of her Immaculate Heart, since what followed the apparition and endured for much of the twentieth century cannot be called a victory. The survival of John Paul II after the assassination attempt and the conversion of Russia after the Act of Consecration prefigure this coming triumph. Already mentioned but worth repeating, at Fatima on 13 May 2010 Pope Benedict said, "We would be mistaken to think that Fatima's prophetic mission is complete... May the seven years which separate us from the centenary of the apparitions hasten the fulfillment of the prophecy of the triumph of the Immaculate Heart of Mary, to the glory of the Most Holy Trinity."

Catholics identify Blessed Mary as queen, seated beside Jesus the King. In particular, this comes from the Gospel of Luke in the passage when Blessed Mary visits her cousin Elizabeth pregnant with John the Baptist:

> When Elizabeth heard Mary's greeting, the infant leaped in her womb, and Elizabeth, filled with the holy Spirit, cried out in a loud voice and said, "Most blessed are you among women, and blessed is the fruit of your womb. And how does this happen to me, that the mother of my Lord should come to me?[141]

Inspired by the Holy Spirit, Elizabeth proclaims Blessed Mary as "mother of my Lord." This Jewish idiom means queen. Because the king had many wives and concubines, usually the mother of the king became

---

[141] USCCB-NAB-Luke 1:39-43 May 20, 2010. <www.usccb.org/nab/bible/luke/luke1.htm>

queen; hence we have Queen Bathsheba on the throne alongside her son King Solomon. Jesus is a king in the line of David. So paraphrasing, Elizabeth is asking, "How is it that the queen comes to me?"

Esther saved her people from annihilation at the hands of the person second to the king, on the thirteenth of the month. Is this a type, a prefiguring, for Jewish Queen Mary delivering her children, her offspring, from Satan (who is said to have been second only to God when he was created) on 13 October 2017?

All public revelation ended with the death of the last apostle but because salvation history is not yet complete, Biblical types have a significant part to play in the second coming of Jesus. From mining the Scriptures and looking at heavenly events in our times such as the Fatima apparition, typology can be seen to indeed be at work and it has much to tell us about future events, including the timings of these events. While some might say the relationship between the thirteenth day of Adar in the book of Esther and the thirteenth day of Fatima is coincidental and cannot possibly be linked over 2600 years, the Bible says:

> Remember the former things, those long ago: I am God, there is no other; I am God, there is none like me. At the beginning I foretell the outcome; in advance, things not yet done. I say that my plan shall stand, I accomplish my every purpose.[142]

One could argue that the thirteenth of Adar is the result of casting lots, which is simple luck. Or is it? Again, from Holy Scriptures:

> When the lot is cast into the lap, its decision depends entirely on the LORD.[143]

In salvation history we can find at least two other significant occurrences of the thirteenth. The survival of the people of God was severely tested nearly two hundred years before the birth of Jesus. The Seleucid Greek Empire took control of Judea and enforced the Hellenization of the territory, including worship of the pagan Greek gods. The Seleucids wanted to assimilate the Jews into their empire and this required destroying any remnant of the Jewish religious culture. In 167 BCE Jewish Temple sacrifice and worship were outlawed, the Jewish

---

[142] USCCB-NAB- Isaiah 46:8b-10, July 13, 2010. <www.usccb.org/nab/bible/isaiah/isaiah46.htm>
[143] USCCB-NAB-Proverbs 16:33

festival celebrations and Holy Sabbaths were declared illegal, and circumcision was forbidden. The Temple was defiled by sacrificing proscribed animals such as pigs on the altars and by erecting statues of Greek gods within the inner sanctuaries. Making the possession of Jewish Holy Scriptures a capital offense impeded the education of future generations of Jews.

The Maccabees, a Jewish rebel army, fought the Seleucids and took control of Judea and reasserted the Jewish religion. The decisive battle between Judas, the Maccabean leader, and Nicanor, general of the Seleucid army, resulted in the death of Nicanor and the triumph of the Jews over their enemies. This battle took place on the thirteenth of Adar.

And earlier we saw how Constantine, in the year 313, after the period known as the Great Persecution of the Church, triumphed under the banner of the cross and issued the Edict of Milan that proclaimed toleration of Christians in the Roman Empire. Under his rule, Christianity became the dominant religion throughout the empire.

The victories of Judas Maccabee and Constantine are milestones in salvation history. In both instances the people of God were under the threat of annihilation, but triumphed.

So many occurrences of the number thirteen make it hard to deny its special relevance in salvation history. This is not numerology. The resounding repetition of the number thirteen throughout salvation history in the triumphs of good over evil, of God over Satan, noticed because of the Fatima apparition, cannot be ignored. Because of Fatima, it is clear that the number thirteen in the Book of Esther is a typological pointer to the timing of events to come, where good ultimately triumphs over evil. *"In the end, my Immaculate Heart will Triumph."* Is Fatima telling us the date of that triumphal end will involve the number thirteen?

Another Number

Blessed Mary appeared at Fatima under the title of Our Lady of the Rosary, and during each of the six apparitions she held a rosary in her hand to emphasize its importance in our prayer life. The full rosary at that time consisted of 153 Hail Mary prayers, and there are 153 days between the first Fatima apparition on 13 May 1917 and the last apparition on October 13, inclusive. The 153 days of Fatima point to the rosary as a means of prayer that will save us. One of the promises made by Blessed Mary to those who regularly recite the rosary: The soul that recommends itself to me by the recitation of the Rosary shall not perish.

The number 153 appears in the Gospel of John:

> *Jesus said to them, "Bring some of the fish you just caught." So Simon Peter went over and dragged the net ashore full of one hundred fifty-three large fish. Even though there were so many, the net was not torn.*[144]

The footnote accompanying this passage is itself intriguing, considering Blessed Mary appeared in 1917:

> The exact number 153 is probably meant to have a symbolic meaning in relation to the apostles' universal mission; Jerome claims that Greek zoologists catalogued 153 species of fish. Or 153 is the sum of the numbers from 1 to 17.

Peter dragging the 153 fish in a net that does not tear provides a type for the Church's salvific power. In the end, the Church, led by Peter and his successors, presents to the Father the elect from throughout the world, "caught" during the Church Age. The net did not tare means none of the elect are lost. From an eschatological perspective, the Holy Father brings to the Father "the catch" of the Church —Jesus established the Church in the world and made its leaders the fishers of men. The fish represent all the peoples saved by following the teachings of the Church guided by the Holy Father, who holds the keys to salvation.

As with most things Catholic, this idea is not new. Saint Augustine taught the number 153 in John's Gospel represented the sum total of all the elect throughout the ages that are saved by following the Gospel of Christ taught through His Church. This is the fullness of the Gentiles. Thus the 153 days of Fatima point in a certain way to the finality of these days.

In Matthew 12:15-21 Jesus quotes the prophet Isaiah's foretelling of the extension of His mission to the Gentiles. He will succeed in His mission and save the elect among the Gentiles.[145] In Romans 11:25, Paul teaches us the Jewish people will recognize Jesus only after the fullness of the Gentiles comes in; that, in God's plan of salvation, Israel's unbelief is being used to spread the faith to the Gentiles.

---

[144] USCCB-NAB-John 21:10-11, June 12, 2010. <www.usccb.org/nab/bible/john/john21.htm>
[145] USCCB-NAB-Matt. 12:15-21, June 12, 2010. <www.usccb.org/nab/bible/matthew/matthew12.htm>

In Luke 21:24, Jesus tells us that Jerusalem will be trampled underfoot by the Gentiles until the times of the Gentiles are fulfilled. The "times of the Gentiles" is a period of indeterminate length separating the destruction of Jerusalem from the cosmic signs accompanying the coming of the Son of Man.[146] This is roughly the same time period as the Age of the Church, the symbolic one thousand years of Revelation 20.

As with the 153 fish in the net, Fatima's time span of 153 days symbolically represents the "times of the Gentiles"—the Age of the Church. According to Scripture, the "time of the Gentiles" ends with the fiery transformation of the cosmos into the new heaven and new earth, and the 153 days of Fatima ended with the fiery descent of the sun. Is the descent of the sun a typological representation of the Last Day? In the end, my Immaculate Heart will triumph. Is the Miracle of the Sun a preview of the triumph of Mary's Immaculate Heart? Does the promised triumph of the Immaculate Heart of Mary literally occur at the end—of the age, on the last day? At Medjugorje, which Our Lady says is the continuation and fulfillment of what she began at Fatima, the Virgin Mary says that Satan's power over the earth will be broken forever with the fulfillment of those apparitions. Theologically, Satan's power ends only at the end of this present world.

Elijah and the Miracle of the Sun

Its meaning is as complex as the miracle is powerful, and it reveals three overlapping eschatological connotations found in the book of Malachi where we read of the sun of justice with its healing rays, and Elijah, and fire:

> For lo, the day is coming...when all the proud and all evildoers will be stubble, And the day that is coming will set them on fire...says the LORD of hosts. But for you who fear my name, there will arise the sun of justice with its healing rays... Lo, I will send you Elijah, the prophet, Before the day of the LORD comes, the great and terrible day[147]

The Passover seder is traditionally connected with the Messianic age. Jews expect Elijah to come to announce the Messiah, and they remember him at their seder meal each year by placing a full cup of wine on the table

---

[146] USCCB-NAB Luke 21:24 footnote 7
[147] USCCB-NAB- Malachi 3:19-23, June 14, 2010. <www.usccb.org/nab/bible/malachi/malachi3.htm>

for him. Later, the door is opened and he is invited in so that he will announce the age of peace.

We know the Elijah who precedes the first coming of Jesus is His cousin John the Baptist, because Jesus told us.[148] Elijah is a type for John the Baptist.

Jesus indicates Elijah will come twice, once before each of His comings, because He said, "Elijah will indeed come and restore all things; but I tell you that Elijah has already come." This means we can expect a typological Elijah before the Last Day. This person will take on the mantle of the prophet, tirelessly warning us to repent and to return to God.

At Fatima Blessed Mary revealed herself as the second typological Elijah through the Miracle of the Sun, which is an antitype to Elijah's calling down fire from heaven on Mount Carmel in a duel against the prophets of the false god Baal. (It is interesting to note that Mount Carmel can be seen from Nazareth, the home of Mary, so she must have looked upon it virtually every day.)

The biblical account of Elijah calling down fire:

Now summon all Israel to me on Mount Carmel, as well as the four hundred and fifty prophets of Baal and the four hundred prophets of Asherah...

So Ahab... had the prophets assemble on Mount Carmel.

Elijah appealed to all the people and said, "How long will you straddle the issue? If the LORD is God, follow him; if Baal, follow him." The people, however, did not answer him. So Elijah said to the people, "I am the only surviving prophet of the LORD, and there are four hundred and fifty prophets of Baal. Give us two young bulls....cut it into pieces, and place it on the wood, but start no fire. I shall prepare the other and place it on the wood, but shall start no fire. You shall call on the name of your gods, and I will call on the name of the LORD. The God who answers with fire is God."

All the people answered, "Agreed!"

Elijah then said to the prophets of Baal, "Choose one young bull and prepare it first, for there are more of you. Call upon your gods, but do not start the fire."

---

[148] Jesus spoke of Elijah in Matthew 17:10-13.

Taking the young bull that was turned over to them, they prepared it and called on Baal from morning to noon, saying, "Answer us, Baal!" But there was no sound, and no one answering... and no one was listening.

Then Elijah said to all the people, "Come here to me." When they had done so, he repaired the altar of the LORD which had been destroyed. When he had arranged the wood, he cut up the young bull and laid it on the wood.

"Fill four jars with water," he said, "and pour it over the holocaust and over the wood." "Do it again," he said, and they did it again. "Do it a third time," he said, and they did it a third time.
The water flowed around the altar, and the trench was filled with the water.

At the time for offering sacrifice, the prophet Elijah came forward and said, "LORD, God of Abraham, Isaac, and Israel, let it be known this day that you are God in Israel and that I am your servant and have done all these things by your command. Answer me, LORD! Answer me, that this people may know that you, LORD, are God and that you have brought them back to their senses."

The LORD'S fire came down and consumed the holocaust, wood, stones, and dust, and it lapped up the water in the trench. Seeing this, all the people fell prostrate and said, "The LORD is God! The LORD is God!"[149]

Comparing this biblical event to the Miracle of the Sun shows the first to be a type for the second:

Elijah:
"You shall call on the name of your gods, and I will call on the name of the LORD. The God who answers with fire is God." All the people answered, "Agreed!"
This means the people would believe in the God who answered with fire.
Blessed Mary:
"In October...I will perform a miracle for all to see and believe."[150]

---

[149] USCCB-NAB-1 Kings 18:19-26,28-39, March 7, 2010.
<www.usccb.org/nab/bible/1kings/1kings18.htm>
[150] Sister Lúcia of Jesus (Lúcia Santos), *Fatima in Lucia's Own Words*, 178.

Elijah asked that his sacrifice be soaked with water, and it was:
"The water flowed around the altar, and the trench was filled with the water."[151]

At Fatima, the crowd that had gathered was soaked with rain:
"The rain ...continued unabated and was now soaking their heads, and drenching them thoroughly."[152]

Elijah called fire down from heaven:
"LORD, God of Abraham, Isaac, and Israel, let it be known this day that you are God ... Answer me, that this people may know that you, LORD, are God and that you have brought them back to their senses."[153]

Lucia described the beginning of the Miracle of the Sun:
"Opening her hands, [Blessed Mary] made them reflect on the sun, and as she ascended, the reflection of her own light continued to be projected on the sun itself."[154] Blessed Mary reflected her own splendor onto the sun, and the sun then "danced" and gave off a dazzling array of colors, but then "the sun...dislodged itself from the firmament, and ...   advanced on the earth, threatening to crush us with the weight of its enormous and fiery mass."[155]

Elijah called fire down onto a water-soaked sacrifice; Blessed Mary called the "fiery mass" of the sun down upon a rain-soaked sacrificial people (Mary had asked the people through her appearance at Fatima to sacrifice themselves by prayer and penance and to "make sacrifices for sinners; for many souls go to hell, because there are none to sacrifice themselves and to pray for them."[156]).

Lastly, the fire called down by Elijah lapped up the water in the trench, leaving it dry. After the descent of the fiery sun, "called" down from the heavens by Blessed Mary, "the people noticed ... the ground and even their clothes were dry."[157]

---

[151] USCCB-NAB-1 Kings 18:35, March 15, 2010. <www.usccb.org/nab/bible/1kings/1kings18.htm>

[152] Martins, *Documents on Fatima & the Memoirs of Sister Lucia,* 214. All rights reserved. Used with permission.

[153] USCCB-NAB-1 Kings 18:36-37

[154] Martins, *Documents on Fatima & the Memoirs of Sister Lucia,* 182.

[155] Ibid,216

[156] Sister Lúcia of Jesus and of the Immaculate Heart, *Fatima in Lucia's Own Words* vol. 1, Ravengate Press, September 2004 - 14th edition, p. 93.

[157] EWTN's Saints and Other Holy People Home, March 15, 2010.
<www.ewtn.com/saintsholy/saints/O/ourladyoffatima.asp>

Along with the sun miracle, Lucia saw visions of Blessed Mary, Jesus, and St. Joseph. Pointedly, the last vision was Our Lady of Mount Carmel, the place Elijah called down the fire: "I saw Our Lady once more, this time resembling Our Lady of Carmel."[158] Elijah intended to turn the fallen people of God back to the Lord. At Fatima, Blessed Mary asked us to stop offending God and to return to Him in prayer and penance.

At Medjugorje, Blessed Mary said the dates associated with her apparitions have significance, so we note it was 24 June 1981, the Feast of John the Baptist aka Elijah, that she first appeared there.

As for the relationship of Our Lady to Elijah and Mount Carmel, it is a long one, too long to explore here. The Carmelite order's patron saint is Blessed Mary. This monastic order began on Mount Carmel around the twelfth century. The Church considers it to be under the special protection of the Blessed Virgin Mary, hence the order's strong Marian devotion. Two distinguished saints—Saint Teresa of Ávila and Saint John of the Cross—established the Discalced Carmelites. Edith Stein is another notable Carmelite; there are many others. Sister Lucia joined the Carmelites on 25 March 1948.

Sister Lucia saw Our Lady of Mount Carmel holding the scapular. The Carmelite Order's original habit consisted of a black and white or brown and white striped mantle— the striping represented the scorch marks the mantle of Elijah received from the fiery chariot as it fell from his shoulders. Their unique garment consisted of a gray scapular—two strips of gray cloth, worn on the breast and back, and fastened at the shoulders. Scapulars had been in existence since the 550s, when the monastic orders came about. The two pieces of cloth joined at the shoulders and hanging down the back and breast had deep spiritual meaning. Our Lord said in the gospels, 'My yoke is sweet and my burden is light.' The act of putting on the scapular was and is a manifestation of dedication and service to God.[159] Tradition holds that the Carmelite Order's scapular was given to St. Simon Stock by the Blessed Virgin Mary herself in 1251, when she appeared to him and promised that all who died clothed in it would not suffer eternal fire. A miniature version of the Carmelite scapular is popular

---

[158] Sister Lúcia of Jesus and of the Immaculate Heart, *Fatima in Lucia's Own Words* vol. 1, Ravengate Press, September 2004 - 14th edition, p. 183
[159] Brown Scapular History, October 21, 2010.
<http://www.freebrownscapular.com/brown_scapular_history.html>

among Catholics and is one of the most popular devotions in the Church.[160]

Both Elijah and Blessed Mary were assumed into Heaven. Also, Elijah was nourished in the desert by an angel (1 Kings 19:4-8) while the Woman is nourished in the desert by God (Rev 12:14). Both Elijah (2 Kings 2:8) and the Ark of the Covenant (Joshua 3), a type for Blessed Mary, part and cross the river Jordan.

The Miracle of the Sun prefigures the Last Day described in the Book of Malachi:

> *Then you will again see the distinction between the just and the wicked;*
> *Between him who serves God, and him who does not serve him.*
> *For lo, the day is coming...when all the proud and all evildoers will... be*
> *set... on fire...says the LORD of hosts...there will arise the sun of justice*
> *with its healing rays;*[161]

When the sun careened towards the crowd, most believed it was the end of the world. Some accepted it peacefully, while others ran and screamed in terror, the difference being the distinction between the just and the wicked. A few of those present were healed of infirmities such as blindness, as if from the sun's rays. When the sun had returned to its proper place, the muddy ground was dry, and their clothes were clean, again, as if from the sun's healing rays. The sun of justice comes on the Day of Justice, preceded by Elijah. The Miracle of the Sun announces that Blessed Mary is Elijah, and the sun miracle is a foretaste of the sun of justice of the Last Day.

The second typological Elijah, Blessed Mary, has come to restore all things.

The Cross Atop the Mountain

In another significant apparition in the early 1960s at Garabandal, Spain, which will be covered later, Blessed Mary appeared as Our Lady of Mount Carmel, yet again connecting herself with Elijah. And there is another connection among the three major twentieth-century apparitions

---

[160] Ibid.
[161] USCCB-NAB-1 Malachi 3:18-21,23

of Fatima, Garabandal, and Medjugorje. At Fatima, Blessed Mary's final appearance was as Our Lady of Mount Carmel, with a scapular hanging on her arm. The vision of the third secret of Fatima has the pope and other religious and lay people climbing a mountain topped with a cross. At Garabandal, Mary appeared as Our Lady of Mount Carmel, again with a scapular on her arm. On one side of the scapular the Garabandal visionary saw a cross, on the other side, a mountain. And at Medjugorje, a major part of a pilgrimage there is to climb Mount Krizevac (in English, Cross Mountain), a mountain topped with a cross. Many signs and wonders have been observed at the cross on that mountain.

Erected in 1933 for the 1950th anniversary of the death and resurrection of Jesus, on 30 August 1984 Our Lady said this regarding the cross on Mount Krizevac:

> *The cross was in God's plan when you built it. These days especially, go up on the mountain and pray at the foot of the cross. I need your prayers.*

According to the visionaries Our Lady prays before that cross:

> *I am often at Krizevac, at the foot of the cross, to pray there. Now I pray to my Son to forgive the world its sins. The world has begun to convert.*[162]

Did the cross on the mountain in the vision of Fatima, together with the cross and mountain on the scapular at Garabandal point to Cross Mountain of Medjugorje, the last apparition of Blessed Mary in history? Were these prophecies of the actual place of the promised period of peace, fulfilled in our time through the Medjugorje apparitions? And does this connect the Warning and Miracle of Garabandal with Medjugorje's secrets?

Recall the vision of the period of peace shown to the Fatima seers:

> *...Other Bishops, Priests, men and women Religious going up a steep mountain, at the top of which there was a big cross.... [the Holy Father knelt] at the foot of the big Cross.... beneath the two arms of the Cross there were two Angels each with a crystal aspersorium in his hand, in which they gathered up the blood of the Martyrs and with it sprinkled the souls that were making their way to God.*

---

[162] Wayne Weible, *The Final Harvest* Revised and Updated. (CMJ Marian Publishers, 2002), 49.

The message of 2 July 2007 given at Medjugorje:

Dear children...Reject your arrogance and kneel down before my Son.... follow my Son and give me your hands so that, together, we may climb the mountain and win. Thank you.

According to Mirjana, Our Lady was referring to the spiritual climb when she spoke of "climbing the mountain." In Lucia's vision of the period of peace (or reconciliation) in the third part of the secret, the splendor of Blessed Mary blocks the flames emanating from the angel's sword, flames that would set the world afire. This grants the people of God time as they struggle to make their way to the cross, aided by the blood of the martyrs sprinkled upon them. The period of peace of the Fatima vision, where Mary blocks the flames, is the apparition of Medjugorje. At Medjugorje pilgrims literally climb the mountain topped with a cross as they try to find their way back to God in this time of apostasy, this time of conversion purchased with the blood of the martyrs of the past century. And all those throughout the world who follow the messages of Medjugorje are also spiritually climbing the mountain to God.

This means the period of reconciliation at Medjugorje is for conversion before the fire from heaven falls, the fire Lucia saw emanating from the angel's sword. The Miracle of the Sun serves as a type for the fire that will come after Medjugorje, making the sun miracle both an antitype of the fire called down by Elijah and a type for the fire to come after Medjugorje. Blessed Mary is restraining it in our present time while the fullness of the Gentiles comes in, but after that it will fall. There is a pre-determined limit to that time, so Our Lady asks us to convert now. And there is a sense of finality to these events; Our Lady says these are her last apparitions, and that through them the power of Satan in the world will be broken forever. This is the final time she will intervene in such a way, because this is the last time it will be needed since Satan will no longer be in the world. Theologically this happens at the end of the age. *In the end, my Immaculate Heart will Triumph.* Putting all of this together, it means the Miracle of the Sun could be a type for the fiery Last Day.

Lastly, the cross atop the mountain is a symbol of the communion of God with His people. Mount Sinai covered with the Shekinah Glory constitutes the earthly presence of God. Mount Sinai is where God spoke to His people through Moses. It is the place where God united to His people, the Israelites, when the blood of the covenant was sprinkled upon them. At Sinai, the people remained at the base, the priestly class could enter a point higher up, but only Moses could enter the top tier of the mountain. This becomes the model for God's Temple, built on another holy mountain, Moriah, the site of Abraham's sacrifice of Isaac. And the Temple in turn becomes the model for the liturgy of the Mass, where man encounters the divine in the Holy Eucharist instituted by Christ at the Last Supper, when He gives His blood in sacrifice for us. At the Mass, we climb the mountain and enter into the divine heavenly realm of God. The cross atop the mountain—symbolizing the sacrifice of Christ upon the altar—and the people climbing the mountain towards God while being sprinkled with the blood of the martyrs is a vision given to us to remind us of the covenant between God and His people. We are reminded again that we are His bride, and therefore we must remain faithful to the ketubah first given to us at Sinai and then renewed in the blood of the New Covenant.

The Consecration of France to the Sacred Heart of Jesus

The consecration of Russia to the Immaculate Heart of Mary parallels the consecration of France to the Sacred Heart of Jesus a few centuries earlier. Recall from our earlier discussion of Fatima:

> Our Lady then said to me: *"The moment has come in which God asks the Holy Father, in union with all the Bishops of the world, to make the consecration of Russia to my Immaculate Heart, promising to save it by this means ..."*
> I gave an account of this to the confessor, who ordered me to write down what Our Lady wanted done. Later, in an intimate communication, Our Lord complained to me, saying:
> *"They did not wish to heed my request...Like the King of France, they will repent and do it, but it will be late. Russia will have already spread her errors throughout the world, provoking wars, and persecutions of the Church: the Holy Father will have much to suffer."*

Our Lord's mention of the King of France refers to the apparitions of the Sacred Heart of Jesus to Saint Margaret Mary in the late 1600s. In 1689, one year before her death, Saint Margaret Mary tried to reach the Sun King, Louis XIV of France, with a message from Jesus that contained four requests. The King was asked to emblazon the Sacred Heart of Jesus on the royal flags and to build a temple in His honor where He would receive the homage of the Court. It was also requested of the king that he make his consecration to the Sacred Heart, and to pledge his authority before the Holy See to obtain a Mass in honor of the Sacred Heart of Jesus.[163] Three consecutive kings ignored the requests until finally, while in prison, King Louis XVI wrote an Act of Consecration and promised that he would complete the three other parts of the request of Our Lord upon being released.[164] For Divine Providence it was now late: Louis XVI was guillotined on 21 January 1793.

Surprisingly, or maybe not surprisingly, we find a parallel between the apparitions at Fatima and the apparitions of St. Margaret Mary. A major aspect of Fatima is the devotion to the Immaculate Heart of Mary. Blessed Mary told Lucia, "Jesus wishes to make use of you to have me acknowledged and loved. He wishes to establish in the world the devotion to my Immaculate Heart."[165] Similarly, Jesus appeared to Sister (now Saint) Margaret Mary to promulgate devotion to His Sacred Heart.

As part of the devotional of the Sacred Heart of Jesus, one attends Mass on nine consecutive first Fridays of the month, and as part of the devotional of the Immaculate Heart of Mary, one attends Mass on five consecutive first Saturdays of the month. Additionally, both Hearts have an Act of Consecration associated with them.

It seems a type of parallelism is in effect here with the unfolding of the devotions to the two Hearts: the request of an Act of Consecration of France to the Sacred Heart of Jesus, and the request of an Act of Consecration of Russia to the Immaculate Heart of Mary. Both requests were accomplished, but late.

As a result of the refusal of King Louis XIV—as well as the refusal of both his son and grandson, King Louis XV and King Louis XVI, respectively—to publicly consecrate France to the Sacred Heart of Jesus, the Protestant and Masonic counter-church successfully carried out the great upheaval known today as the French Revolution.[166]

---

[163] Bougaud, Monseigneur, *Revelations of the Sacred Heart to Blessed Margaret Mary, and the History of Her Life* (New York: Benziger Brothers, 1890), 268-269, accessed June 23, 2010, www.archive.org/stream/revelationsofthe00bouguoft#page/n271/mode/2up

[164] Ibid, 310-312, accessed June 23, 2010, www.archive.org/stream/revelationsofthe00bouguoft#page/n313/mode/2up

[165] Martins, *Documents on Fatima & the Memoirs of Sister Lucia*, 438.

[166] Brother Michel de la Sainte Trinité, *The Whole Truth About Fatima*, retrieved June 28, 2010. <http://www.catholicvoice.co.uk/fatima2/ch2-7.htm>

Long before the French Revolution, France had divided society into three estates: the First Estate (clergy); the Second Estate (nobility); and the Third Estate (commoners). The king was not considered a member of any estate because the French considered their king to be God's representative over the nation. Jesus made His request to the king of France through Saint Margaret Mary Alacoque on 17 June 1689.[167] On 17 June 1789, exactly one hundred years to the day from when Saint Margaret Mary had written down the great designs of Heaven for the king, the Third Estate rose up and proclaimed itself a national assembly, stripping King Louis XVI of his power.[168] A few years later, imprisoned, the king wrote his Act of Consecration, promising to complete the other parts of the act once released. He was publicly beheaded before he could do it. The Act of Consecration was made at the last moment, too late to change the outcome. In a brief but extremely violent shock to its society, the French monarchy ended and the nation started a transformation to a secular society. The Church was persecuted during the upheaval; many clergy were executed and many churches were closed during the first ten years of the revolution. Knowing all of this was coming, exactly one hundred years beforehand Jesus offered a remedy—devotion to His Sacred Heart.

Looking at the period of the second requested consecration, which began in 1917 with Fatima, a similar but more forceful transformation occurred in the nation of Russia. The Tsar was executed, and a heavily Christian Russia rapidly changed into an atheistic communist state. This started around the time of the October Miracle of the Sun. Christian persecution in Russia began in 1918 and it continued until 1985. Importantly, this transformation was not confined to Russia. Blessed Mary said Russia would spread its errors (a pseudo-religion of man as god, and abortion, among others) throughout the world. Knowing what was coming for Russia and the world, Blessed Mary offered the remedy of devotion to Her Immaculate Heart.

This is all to say that we should note Jesus' mentioning the king of France to Sister Lucia and especially note that exactly one hundred years to the day of His request for the consecration the king of France fell, and the nation degenerated into anarchy and religious persecution. Does this set a time frame for the prophecies of Fatima? Our Lady foretold that Fatima ends with the triumph of her Immaculate Heart. Will this take place one

---

[167] Bougaud, *Revelations of the Sacred Heart to Blessed Margaret Mary*, 267, accessed June 23, 2010, www.archive.org/stream/revelationsofthe00bouguoft#page/n269/mode/2up
[168] Brother Michel de la Sainte Trinité, *The Whole Truth About Fatima*, retrieved June 28, 2010.

hundred years after the Fatima apparitions ceased on 13 October 1917? Is 13 October 2017 the day of her triumph?

The Jubilee Year of the Messiah

The concept of the Jubilee is a special year of remission of sins and universal pardon. It is a joyful time. According to the Book of Leviticus, a Jubilee year occurs every fifty years:

Seven weeks of years shall you count—seven times seven years—so that the seven cycles amount to forty-nine years. Then, on the tenth day of the seventh month let the trumpet resound; on this, the Day of Atonement, the trumpet blast shall re-echo throughout your land. This fiftieth year you shall make sacred by proclaiming liberty in the land for all its inhabitants. It shall be a jubilee for you.[169]

In a Jubilee year, slaves and captives are freed, debts are forgiven, each returns to the land of his family, and the kindness and mercy of God are apparent.

Elijah said in the last jubilee the son of David will come.[170] Jesus began His ministry by quoting Isaiah's words (a description of a time of jubilee):

"The Spirit of the Lord is upon me, because he has anointed me to bring glad tidings to the poor. He has sent me to proclaim liberty to captives and recovery of sight to the blind, to let the oppressed go free, and to proclaim a year acceptable to the Lord."

Rolling up the scroll, he handed it back to the attendant and sat down, and the eyes of all in the synagogue looked intently at him. He said to them, "Today this scripture passage is fulfilled in your hearing."

We have already seen that the prophecies of the Messiah in Malachi and elsewhere refer to both comings of Jesus, so the Messiah is expected to return in a Jubilee year.

Nobody is sure when the first jubilee year occurred, and consequently nobody knows the years of Jubilee. This is one reason why Jewish people

---

[169] USCCB-NAB-Leviticus 25:8-11, November 12, 2010.
<www.usccb.org/nab/bible/leviticus/leviticus25.htm>
[170] Babylonian Talmud: Sanhedrin 97, January 31, 2011.
<halakhah.com/sanhedrin/sanhedrin_97.html#PARTb>

have not observed the regulations for the Jubilee year for many centuries. However, if we could somehow drop onto a jubilee "timeline," we could traverse forward fifty years at a time, knowing one of those jubilee years would be the year of the Messiah's return. It so happens we can do just that.

In 1217, the Jewish Rabbi Judah Ben Samuel prophesied about the final ten Jubilees before the start of the Messianic Kingdom. An article in the March 2008 issue of Israel Today explains:

> Some 800 years ago in Germany, Rabbi Judah Ben Samuel ... prophesied that the Ottoman Turks would conquer Jerusalem and rule the Holy City for "eight jubilee years." A biblical jubilee year consists of 50 years. Fifty multiplied by eight equals 400 years. Afterwards, according to Ben Samuel, the Ottomans would be driven out of Jerusalem, which would remain a no-mans land for one jubilee year. In the tenth jubilee year, Jerusalem would return to the Jewish people and then the Messianic end times would begin. According to Leviticus 25, the nation is reunited with its land in the year of Jubilee.[171]

In 1517, Sultan Selim of the Ottoman Empire captured Jerusalem from the Mamelukes. Then, the Ottoman Turks reigned over Jerusalem until British General Edmund Allenby defeated them exactly eight jubilee years later, in 1917.[172] During the ninth jubilee year, from 1917 to 1967, Jerusalem was a no-man's-land, as predicted by Ben Samuel. In fact, because of the constant fighting, both Israelis and Jordanians referred to it as the no-man's land. In 1967, the Israelis captured East Jerusalem during the Six Day War and "the city returned to the Jewish people after nearly two millennia. After that the countdown for the Messianic age began."[173]

> According to this timeline, it is possible that 2017 or 2018 will be a decisive year for Israel because it will be 70 years after 1947, the U.N. decision for the establishment of Israel and 50 years after the unification of Jerusalem...these numbers have Biblical significance: 50 is the number of unification (for example between Passover and

---

[171] Schneider, Ludwig. "Israel: Between Mysticism and Reality." *Israel Today*, March 2008: 18. Retrieved May 5, 2010 from website <issuu.com/ryaninzion/docs/israel_today_march_2008/18>. Used with permission.
[172] Schneider, "Israel: Between Mysticism and Reality."
[173] Ibid.

Pentecost) and 70, according to Daniel 9, is the number of fulfillment. So 50 and 70 represent the beginning and the end.[174] Concerning this prophecy, it is also interesting to note the Jewish festival of Hanukkah. After defeating the Turks, General Allenby dismounted from his horse and reverently walked into the holy city of Jerusalem through the Jaffa Gate, not wanting to outdo Jesus on His donkey. It was the feast of Hanukkah.

Briefly, Hanukkah commemorates the re-consecration of the Temple after its desecration by the Seleucids circa 160 BCE. For the rededication, special attention was given to lighting the Menorah because if symbolizes the Light of God. Only ritually pure olive oil could be used, but there was only enough to keep the Menorah lit for one day but the oil supply lasted eight days, enough time for a new supply to be prepared. All those looking at the flame on the second day were amazed, and believed they were witnessing a sign from God. And it was on the second day of the feast of Hanukkah that General Allenby walked into Jerusalem. His conquering of the holy city was an important event on a significant date in salvation history.

Prior to the conquest of Jerusalem, the situation in the land of Israel was grim. The Ottoman Turks oppressed the Jewish community. Thousands of Jews were exiled to Alexandria, Egypt, then under British control. In March 1917, Djemal Pasha, the local Turkish governor, ordered the deportation of all Jews in the Jaffa region and threatened a wholesale massacre against them. Before the war, 55,000 Jews resided in Jerusalem; by 1917, due to persecution, just 24,000 remained.[175]

But the tide turned when Allenby defeated the Turkish army. The victory started a chain of events that paved the way for the return of the Jews to the land and the re-birth of the nation of Israel. Anticipating Allenby's victory over the Turkish army at Jerusalem, Great Britain issued the Balfour Declaration on 2 November 1917:

His Majesty's government view with favour the establishment in Palestine of a national home for the Jewish people, and will use their best endeavors to facilitate the achievement of this object, it being clearly understood that nothing shall be done which may prejudice

---

[174] Ibid.
[175] "Chanukah 1917",Our Jerusalem.com, December 19, 2011.
<www.ourjerusalem.com/history/story/chanukah-1917.html>

the civil and religious rights of existing non-Jewish communities in Palestine, or the rights and political status enjoyed by Jews in any other country.

Foreign Secretary Arthur James Balfour sent a letter to Baron Rothschild, one of the leaders of the Jewish community in Great Britain, who in turn passed it to the leaders of the British Zionists.

So began the return of the Jews to the land. On 29 November 1947, the United Nations General Assembly voted in favor of a partition plan for the region that created the State of Israel.

According to the Ben Samuel prophecy 1917 is a jubilee year, and this is borne out by the Book of Leviticus which says a nation is reunited with its land in the year of Jubilee. The "times of the Gentiles" in the city of Jerusalem ended in 1967, the ninth jubilee year of the prophecy.

The tenth jubilee year is 2017, and also the specific jubilee year, according to Rabbi Ben Samuel's prophecy, when the Messiah returns.

Chapter 13
Time, Times, and a Half Time Redux

At this point we have discovered God gave Satan one century to test the Church, and he chose the twentieth century. The seers of Medjugorje say it extends past what we consider the "official" end date of 31 December 2000. We previously created a graphical illustration of the end times period of the "time, times, and a half time":

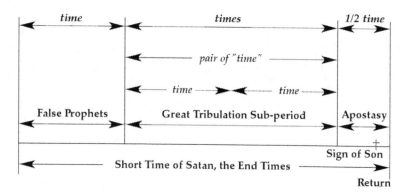

We also determined the expression "time, and times, and half a time" means three and a half units of time proportioned by the ratio 1:2:0.5. If we knew the total length of time involved, using simple algebra and this ratio we could determine the length for the unit of time and use that to calculate the length for "times" and "half time" as well.

We do know the total length of time involved. The twentieth century began on 1 January 1901. From our previous discussions, the year 2017 and in particular the day 13 October 2017 seems to be a significant milestone in salvation history, so it will be used for the end date. Using a date calculator[176], we find the length of time from 1 January 1901 to 13 October 2017 to be approximately 116.75 years.

The length of time is actually 116 years, 9 months, and 13 days. Nine months out of twelve is 0.75 years. This leads to the question of granularity. Should we try to include the days? Fatima spanned six apparitions of Blessed Mary over a period of five months. Also, an angel appeared before Blessed Mary did. What specific day should be used for Fatima in any date analysis? Or is the year 1917 sufficient? The question becomes one of exactitude: what degree of precision should we use? The answer cannot be given with certainty.

Let us use algebra to find the length for the unit of time:

With X equal to one unit of time, from the ratio 1:2:0.5 we can solve the equation:

$$X + 2X + 0.5X = 116.75 \text{ years}$$
$$3.5X = 116.75$$
$$X = 33.3 \text{ years}$$

So "time" is 33.3 years. This number is interesting in itself, since it is symbolic of the Holy Trinity, and also approximates the length of time Jesus walked the earth.

The "times" is 2X or 66.6 years. This of course is the famous "mark of the beast" of Revelation. It is noteworthy that these years cover the most violent sub-period of the short time granted Satan. Jesus described it as a time of Great Tribulation, where *"they will hand you over to persecution, and they will kill you."*[177] On the timeline it spans much of the middle of the twentieth century, which covers persecutions of Christians inside the Soviet Union, World War II, Hitler's Final Solution, the gulags, famines, Mao's persecutions, and the proxy wars of the Cold War.

The "half time" is 0.5X, about 16.7 years. With all three numbers, the end points for each sub-period can be plotted on the timeline:

---

[176] For example, one found at this website: www.timeanddate.com/date/duration.html
[177] USCCB-NAB-Matthew 24:9, June 3, 2010. <www.usccb.org/nab/bible/matthew/matthew24.htm>

First sub-period: January 1, 1901 to May 1934
Second sub-period: May 1934 to January 1, 2001
Third sub-period: January 1, 2001 to October 13, 2017

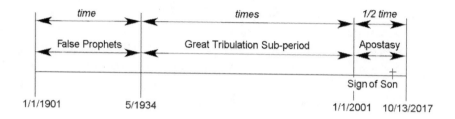

Aside from January 2001 being the start of both a century and a millennium, nothing else is apparent from these dates. There is nothing that says the end times sub-periods have to go in the order of time, times, and a half time. Let's try reversing the order and use a half time, times, and time (this changes the length of time for each sub-period, but the order of events given by Jesus in Matthew 24 remains the same—false prophets, then great tribulation followed by apostasy):

(time) Third sub-period: 1984 to October 13, 2017 (2017.75-33.3=1984.4)
(times) Second: 1917 to 1984   (1984.4-66.6 =1917.8)
(1/2 time) First: January 1, 1901 to 1917   (1917.8-16.7 =1901.1)

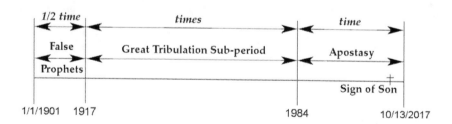

The year 1917 is the year of the Fatima apparitions. The year 1984 is the year when Pope John Paul II completed the Act of Consecration of Russia to the Immaculate Heart of Mary, requested through the Fatima apparitions. And of course October 13 is the anniversary date of Fatima's Miracle of the Sun and a possible type for something greater, such as the

Triumph of the Immaculate Heart of Mary or more. Key events from the Fatima apparition define the sub-periods of the timeline, the same timeline we developed earlier from the Olivet Discourse in the Gospel of Matthew, Revelation chapter 20, and the Book of Daniel:

> *That will be a time of great distress, unparalleled since nations first came into existence. When that time comes, your own people will be spared—all those whose names are found written in the Book. Of those who are sleeping in the Land of Dust, many will awaken, some to everlasting life, some to shame and everlasting disgrace. Many will roam about, this way and that, and wickedness will continue to increase.*
>
> *' How long until these wonders take place?'*
>
> *'A time and two times, and half a time; and all these things will come true, once the crushing of the holy people's power is over.'* [178]

Daniel also says:

> *And that the power of the other beasts was taken away: and that times of life were appointed them for a time, and a time.* [179]

Some beasts of the time of the end will live for *a time, and a time*—a pair of times—and this matches the pair of times of 66.6 years on the timeline. At Fatima, Our Lady showed the children a vision of godless men leading the world into war and ruin, and she said this would last until the Act of Consecration and Reparation Saturdays. With the consecration of 1984, the "times" of the beasts, the godless men spoken of by Our Lady, came to an end.

At Garabandal, Our Lady said that after the reign of Pope John XXIII, there would be three more popes and then it would be the end of the times, but not the end of the world. [180] It is apparent from the timeline that Blessed Mary was referring to the "times" part of "time, times, and a half time"—the great tribulation sub-period—when she used the word "times." John Paul II was the third pope after John XXIII, and he ended the "times" by enacting the consecration.

The number thirty-three is associated with purification. According to Leviticus 12:4, a woman spends thirty-three days in purification after giving birth to a son. There is a period of exactly thirty-three months

---

[178] Daniel–Chapter 12:1b,4,6b,7b–Bible, June 19, 2010. <www.catholic.org/bible/book.php?id=34>

[179] Douay-Rheims Catholic Bible, Prophecy Of Daniel Chapter 7:12, June 21,2010. <www.drbo.org/chapter/32007.htm>

[180] "The Three Popes and Garabandal: Revisited Again in Light of the Passing of His Holiness Pope John Paul II", June 25, 2010. <www.ourlady.ca/info/THE_THREE_POPES_AND_GARAB.htm>

between the celebrated anniversary of Mary's Medjugorje apparitions on 25 June 1981 until the Act of Consecration of Russia on 25 March 1984. In the first thirty-three months of the apparitions, the messages at Medjugorje served as "teaching" lessons and for explaining the general purpose of the Blessed Virgin's appearance in the village.[181] Bold signs and wonders occurred in the entire area during that time, and Blessed Mary guided and instructed the parish for its role in future events. For example, after the villagers saw the cross on Mount Krizevac transform itself into a cross of light and then into a silhouette of Our Lady, Blessed Mary said, "*All these signs are designed to strengthen your faith...*"[182]

To the astonishment of the local inhabitants, Our Lady said their remote village would become a place of pilgrimage and she encouraged the people to open their doors to the pilgrims, reminding them that they will come seeking God. At the beginning of March 1984, Our Lady said:

> *Dear children! I have chosen this parish in a special way and I wish to lead it. I am guarding it in love and I want everyone to be mine. Thank you for having responded tonight. I wish you always to be with me and my Son in ever greater numbers.*

On 12 April 1984 Blessed Mary said, "*...I and my Son have a special plan for this parish.*"

And on 9 June 1984 Our Lady alluded to the role of the parish as the wellspring of the heavenly messages intended to turn the world back to God, when she said:

> *Dear children! Tomorrow night pray for the Spirit of Truth! Especially, you from the parish. Because you need the Spirit of Truth to be able to convey the messages just the way they are, neither adding anything to them, nor taking anything whatsoever way from them, but just the way I said them.*

This message was given shortly after the consecration requested at Fatima was enacted. This was because from the time of the consecration onwards the messages are directed towards the world, because Our Lady of Fatima promised a period of peace (reconciliation) for the world after the

---

[181] A Brief History of the Messages, April 6, 2010.
<www.medjugorjeweible.com/images/messages.htm>
[182] Rene Laurentin and R. Lejeune, *Messages and Teachings of Mary at Medjugorje*, 168.

consecration was completed, and Medjugorje is that period of reconciliation. The change in the salutation Blessed Mary uses to start her messages shows this:

> In Mary's appearances to the seers prior to March, 1984, the beginning salutation was usually: Praise be Jesus. In leaving the children, the ending words were usually: Go in the Peace of God. Beginning in March, 1984, the messages were usually given for the parish (and the world), and the opening salutation from the Madonna was usually: Dear Children! In leaving, Mary almost always thanked those involved with: Thank you for having responded to my call.[183]

After exactly thirty-three months, on 25 March 1984, John Paul II consecrated Russia and the world to the Immaculate Heart of Mary, as requested through the apparition of Fatima. And on this day, Our Lady gave her one-thousandth message:

> *Rejoice with me and my angels because a part of my plan has already been realized. Many have been converted, but many do not want to be converted. Pray.*

This points to the thousand years of Revelation chapter 20, and the thousand years are not to be taken literally; they symbolize the long period of time between the chaining up of Satan (a symbol for Christ's resurrection-victory over death and the forces of evil) and the end of the world.[184]

> *[The angel] overpowered... Satan, and chained him up for a thousand years... At the end of that time he must be released, but only for a short while.*[185]

Satan was granted one century, the twentieth, and that ended on 31 December 2000. However, Our Lady has told us through a message to seer Marija on 1 January 2001 that although his century is over, he remains unchained:

---

[183] Ibid, 148.
[184] USCCB-NAB-Revelation 20, Footnote 1, June 25, 2010.
<www.usccb.org/nab/bible/revelation/revelation20.htm#foot1>
[185] Catholic Online, Revelation Chapter 20:2-3, July 8, 2010.
<www.catholic.org/bible/book.php?id=73>

In a special way now when Satan is free from chains, I invite you to consecrate yourselves to my Heart and to the Heart of my Son.

From the timeline, it seems the events associated with the Medjugorje apparition (which is actually a part of Fatima since it is the fulfillment of the Fatima apparition) will end on 13 October 2017, thirty-three years after the Act of Consecration. Blessed Mary's message to Mirjana on 2 September 2010:

Dear children, I am beside you because I desire to help you to overcome trials, which this time of purification puts before you. My children, one of those is not to forgive and not to ask for forgiveness.

The meaning of the word time in the message is layered — on the deeper level it refers to the eschatological "time" of time, times and a half time, and Our Lady calls this *time* one of purification. We saw from Leviticus the number thirty-three is associated with the amount of time for purification after a woman gives birth to a son.

All of these numbers and word choices such as "chains" and "purification" are signs of the times, and are given to help us understand the meaning behind Our Lady's appearances at Fatima, Garabandal, and Medjugorje.

The visionaries say there are no coincidences with the apparitions. For example (and intriguingly), the last apparition of Blessed Mary on the earth is at St. James Parish, and reportedly her first apparition was to the Apostle James in Zaragoza, Spain. We've come full circle.

Chapter 14
The End Times — The Twentieth Century

In Part I we learned the Gospel message of Jesus had been preached throughout the world at the start of the twentieth century.

And this gospel of the kingdom will be preached throughout the world as a witness to all nations, and then the end will come.[186]

We also discovered God gave Satan one century to test the Church and he chose the twentieth century. It would be useful to concisely review the history of the twentieth century through the lens of salvation history. One cannot overestimate the significance of the Fatima apparitions in that history. Fatima has been shown to be the key that unlocks the Olivet Discourse and the phrase "time, times, and a half time". The "Message of Fatima" document released by the Church in June 2000 indicated the important role of Fatima: "The twentieth century was one of the most crucial in human history, with its tragic and cruel events culminating in the assassination attempt on the [Pope]. Now a veil is drawn back on a series of events which make history and interpret it in depth, in a spiritual perspective alien to present-day attitudes, often tainted with rationalism."[187]

---

[186] USCCB-NAB-Matthew 24:14, June 30, 2010. <www.usccb.org/nab/bible/matthew/matthew24.htm>
[187] "The Message of Fatima," March 8, 2010.
<www.vatican.va/roman_curia/congregations/cfaith/documents/rc_con_cfaith_doc_20000626_message
-fatima_en.html>

The opening act of the Short Time of Satan began around 1901 at the beginning of the twentieth century. Satan through his followers used the years 1901 to 1914, prior to World War I, to not too subtly guide mankind away from the teachings of Jesus.

See that no one deceives you. For many will come in my name, saying, 'I am the Messiah,' and they will deceive many.[188]

The first years of the century were a period of rapid change that saw the onrush of modernism. First planted in the mid-1800s, modernism reached full bloom in the early 1900s. Modernists discarded common nineteenth-century thinking, and many of them jettisoned the idea of a compassionate, all-powerful Creator. While it can be argued that not every modernist movement rejected religion or all aspects of nineteenth-century thought, it is true that all modernists questioned the tightly held beliefs of the previous era. Modernism shifts the emphasis away from the power of God and towards the power of human beings to create, change, and improve their environment through scientific experimentation, knowledge, and technology.

Pope Leo XIII and Pope Pius X both fought the rise of modernism early in the twentieth century. Dogmas are the teachings of the Catholic Church that its members must believe. These are authoritative teachings integral to the faith that do not change. God does not change and therefore His truth that He has revealed to us cannot change. An example of a dogma is the Ascension of Jesus. Modernism is the antithesis of dogmas because its basic tenet is that dogmas can change over time, and this is what makes it unique. Previously, there had never been a heresy like it throughout the long history of the Church.

Prior to Modernism, a person who taught or believed something outside of the teachings of the Church—a heretic—would claim either a personal divine revelation or a divine inspiration that enabled him to know new but contradictory ideas about God heretofore unknown by the Church. In such cases, it was relatively easy to determine the person to be in schism with the Church, and upon refusal to recant the person was excommunicated—ejected from the corporate Church body. Prior to Modernism, a person either conformed to the teachings of the Church, or did not. One was either inside or outside the Church.

---

[188] Matthew 24:5

With the idea that doctrines evolve, the modernist could claim the teachings of the Church and his new, contradictory beliefs were equally correct relative to their time and place in history. This concept permits virtually any new belief the modernist wants to follow, and precisely for this reason Modernism was called the synthesis of all heresies by Pope Pius X in the early 1900s.

One of the tools used by modernists to "change" Church teachings is Scriptural interpretation. The modernist renders new interpretations to the text, twisting it into saying what he wants it to say. By this means modernists argue that certain passages in the holy texts don't say what the Church has always held them to mean. To counter this, in 1893 Pope Leo XIII released the encyclical *Providentissimus Deus*, which said Biblical criticism was legitimate only if it was pursued in a spirit of faith. In 1903 Leo established a Pontifical Biblical Commission to oversee those studies and ensure they were conducted with respect for the Catholic doctrines on the inspiration and interpretation of scripture.

Moral standards greatly changed during the twentieth century. Prior to the twentieth century a Catholic would have had to break with his faith to indulge in some of the practices of his contemporaries. But by leaning on Modernism, the theory that dogmas can change, the Catholic can partake in previously immoral acts without being concerned about acting in a manner contrary to the faith. We see this today with Catholic politicians who support abortion by claiming the Church has forgotten that at one time in its ancient past it accepted abortion in certain circumstances, a claim which is demonstrably false but nonetheless asserted by modernists as they seek cover from the threat of excommunication.

Pope Pius X, who succeeded Leo, was the first to identify Modernism as a movement. He totally and unequivocally condemned it. Deeply concerned by Modernism's ability to deceive its followers into believing themselves to be strict Catholics while behaving in a way markedly different from Catholic teaching, the Vatican in 1907 published *Lamentabili Sane Exitu*. This defined sixty-five propositions of the Modernist Heresy, and condemned all of it. Later that year, Pius X wrote the encyclical *Pascendi dominici gregis*. This was followed in 1910 with the compulsory Oath Against Modernism for all Catholic bishops, priests and teachers.

To make a house collapse, weaken its foundation. Through Modernism Satan attacks the foundations of the church, especially the truth of the Holy Scriptures. Pope Paul VI warned in the 1960s the smoke of Satan had entered into the Church through the cracks. In a recent message from

Blessed Mary at Medjugorje on 25 May 2010, she warned about the dangers of modernism:

Dear children ... Satan ... does not sleep and through modernism diverts you and leads you to his way. Therefore, ... love God above everything and live His commandments. In this way, your life will have meaning and peace will rule on earth.

Early modernists who thrived prior to the beginning of the twentieth century include Karl Marx, founder of atheistic communism, and philosopher Friedrich Nietzsche. Nietzsche is the author the infamous quote: "Gods too decompose. God is dead. God remains dead. And we have killed him." And another quote of his that foreshadowed relativism, which is the denial of the existence of any absolute truths: "You have your way. I have my way. As for the right way, the correct way, and the only way, it does not exist."

Nietzsche's ideas were popular in the years prior to World War I, as was the idea of nihilism. By "God is dead", Nietzsche meant mankind's advances in science led to increased secularization of Europe, the cradle of Christianity. This effectively "killed" the Christian God, who had served as the basis for meaning and value in the West for more than a thousand years. With God "dead," nihilism followed. Nihilism argues that life is without meaning, purpose, or intrinsic value, that there is no reason to exist. Moral nihilists extend that to morality by asserting that absolute morality does not exist, and that traditional moral values are found only in theory and not in reality. What Nietzsche was saying, basically, is that man, with the improvements in his life brought about through the fruits of his own science and innovation had created a "good life" here on earth and thus no longer had need of the idea of a Creator-being. Prior to this, the majority of people lived at a subsistence level, struggling from day to day. In such a world, the Christian paradisiacal heaven as a final, just reward for all the earthly toils gave life meaning, and for many death, while sorrowful, was seen as a release from a hellish life of struggle. But as the quality of life improved and the struggle to simply survive eased for the Christian West at the beginning of the twentieth century, the idea of death as a release began to diminish, and then gradually to reverse. People began to think life was "pretty good." Newspapers, department stores, the phonograph and motion pictures, the telephone, cars, the telegraph, and the airplane—all of these rapidly changed daily life in the Christian West. One could say that to a small degree, through science man created an artificial, reduced facsimile of heaven. This is not to say that improvements to the quality of life are immoral or undesirable, but it is alarming that these are used in support of modernistic ideas that weaken the people's faith.

The seeds of the final great deception of our day, which mirror those of the first great deception of Satan to Adam and Eve, began in the early twentieth century; simply stated, man can be like God, and indeed man is God. It is noteworthy that at the beginning of the history of man, and at the possible end of the history of man, at a time just prior to a "new heaven and a new earth," the deception is the same.

In his book, *The Vertigo Years: Europe, 1900–1914,* Philipp Blom claims that everything that was to become important in the twentieth century, "from quantum physics to women's emancipation, from abstract art to space travel, from communism to fascism to the consumer society, from industrialized slaughter to the power of the media" was already evident in the first fifteen years of the twentieth century.

Nation will rise against nation, and kingdom against kingdom[189]

Those first relatively tranquil years were followed in 1914 with the shocking brutality of World War I, which lasted until 1918 and involved most of the world's great powers. From a restive peace, nation suddenly rose against nation. The details of World War I do not concern us here. From the perspective of the century being one of warfare between an unleashed Satan and the City of God, the major events to note during WWI are the apparitions at Fatima, the Balfour Declaration, and the transformation, virtually overnight, of Russia into an officially atheistic state. All of these major historical events happened in 1917. Fatima and the rise of communism in revolutionary Russia are inextricably linked because Blessed Mary mentioned Russia by name and spoke of the errors and trials she (Russia) would bring upon the world. In the Balfour Declaration the government of Great Britain, one of the world's most powerful nations, declared to the leading Jewish families of the day their decision to promote the establishment of a national homeland for the Jewish people in Palestine. This was a monumental action in light of biblical prophecy and the nation of Israel. Any one of these three events individually would be the most notable event of the year and a milestone in world history. For all three to happen in the same year sets 1917 apart.

---

[189] Matthew 24:7a

The appearance of Blessed Mary at Fatima in 1917 was significant in that it announced to the City of God Satan's chosen instrument of persecution against it.

Then they will hand you over to persecution, and they will kill you.[190]

After World War I, an impoverished Russian state began its slow climb up the ranks of nations to eventually become the world's second most powerful nation—and the first most evil. Renamed the Union of Soviet Socialist Republics, between the two world wars Joseph Stalin pushed industrialization onto the once chiefly agrarian nation. World War II saw the rise of Hitler and the slaughter of some six million of God's chosen people, the Jews, as well as five million others, and this does not take into account the war dead. The Soviet Union emerged from World War II in control of Christian Eastern Europe, forcing it to become officially atheist. The USSR was by now very powerful.

You will hear of wars and reports of wars[191]

The Cold War began and the US and its allies struggled to keep the Soviet Union at bay as she relentlessly tried by force of arms to spread her error of atheism around the world. The Soviets aided Mao as he seized power in China, and Mao in turn aided North Korea, encouraging it to invade the south. Vietnam and Cuba fell under the communist yoke, as did several African nations. In 1962, the world stood on the brink of nuclear annihilation as the US and the USSR faced off over nuclear missiles in Cuba, but the cool-headed President John F. Kennedy, the only Catholic ever elected president, led the world safely through the crisis. Throughout the Cold War, the West was probed worldwide for weakness of arms and weakness of will. Out of necessity, the US and its allies formed the North Atlantic Treaty Organization (NATO) as a bulwark against atheistic communist aggression.

The Soviet Union's counter to NATO was the Warsaw Pact, which united by treaty the communist countries of Eastern Europe and the USSR, with the governments of those countries acting as puppet governments installed by the Soviets. But in 1978 for the first time in history, a Pole was elected pope. With the USSR threatening the NATO countries of the West,

---

[190] Matthew 24:9a
[191] USCCB-NAB-Matthew 24:6a

this development was very significant. Poland was and is a devoutly Catholic country, but was being led by a puppet atheistic government established through Soviet might. The Polish people rallied to the Polish pope and the Solidarity movement was born and grew.

When you see the desolating abomination... standing in the holy place[192]

Intimidated, the Soviet Union devised a plot to assassinate the pope and on 13 May 1981, in Saint Peter's Square, Mehmet Ali Agca severely wounded Pope John Paul II. The professional assassin fired an exploding bullet at the pope's head from point-blank range but missed because at the exact moment he pulled the trigger, the pope bent over. It has been said that the pope bent over to bless a little girl and the Our Lady of Fatima pin she wore that day in honor of the Feast of Our Lady of Fatima. Agca fired several more times, hitting the Pope in the abdomen. Doctors later said the bullet took an unexplainable curving path through his body, missing vital organs and arteries by millimeters. The pope later said that "it was a mother's hand that guided the bullet's path" and in his throes the pope halted at the threshold of death. (Pope John Paul II, Meditation from the Policlinico Gemelli to the Italian Bishops, 13 May 1994).[193]

The pope recuperated, and because he was shot on the feast of Our Lady of Fatima, he decided to read the church files on Fatima, becoming convinced as he did so that he must make the Act of Consecration requested by Our Lady of Fatima in order to save mankind. And so one year later, on 13 May 1982, he made the Act of Consecration at Fatima, Portugal, but because he did not do it in union with the bishops, as requested, the consecration was not accepted. In 1983, setting an example of the forgiveness we are called to offer, John Paul II forgave his would-be assassin. Meanwhile, in the United States, President Reagan was moving forward on improving the US military and began to talk of a "star wars" missile shield that would protect the country from incoming nuclear missiles. This raised great alarm in the halls of the Kremlin because the nascent Star Wars defense plan had the potential to render the Russian nuclear arsenal impotent. We now know from documents released after the Cold War that the Soviet Union in its effort to keep pace with US military growth, had bankrupted its economy. Hence, in 1985 the USSR

---

[192] Matthew 24:15
[193] The Message of Fatima, March 6, 2010.
<www.vatican.va/roman_curia/congregations/cfaith/documents/rc_con_cfaith_doc_20000626_message
-fatima_en.html>

was not in a financial position to invest in advanced technologies such as Star Wars. The only choice would be to use the arsenal before it became obsolete and that is what the hardliners inside the Soviet Union's political and military camps decided.

This provides support to Sister Lucia's statement that a nuclear war would have begun in 1985 had the pope not made the Act of Consecration. When one looks at the situation that existed between the West and the USSR at that time, this is easy to believe.

> *And if those days had not been shortened, no one would be saved; but for the sake of the elect they will be shortened.*[194]

But on 25 March 1984, John Paul II finally enacted the consecration requested by God through Blessed Mary at Fatima in 1917. This act was of historical importance for several reasons. First, it shortened the ongoing Great Tribulation, thus preventing the impending nuclear war of 1985 that Sister Lucia said would have occurred. Undoubtedly, that war would have led to the destruction of mankind. Jesus said that had the tribulation not been shortened, no one would be saved.[195] In an interview with Cardinal Ricardo Vidal in 1993, Sr. Lucia commented on the secret prophecy:

> The triumph of the Immaculate Heart of Mary also refers to [her victory over] the errors that were being spread by Russia. The Consecration of 1984 prevented an atomic war that would have occurred in 1985.[196]

The appearance of Blessed Mary at Fatima in 1917 took place to warn us about the great tribulation to come upon the world through Russia and also to give us a remedy to shorten that tribulation via the Act of Consecration of Russia. And while the consecration was done late, it was done. Had we listened to Blessed Mary and made sacrifices and penances, including the First Saturday devotions she mentioned at Fatima, no doubt a strong inspiration would have come from the Holy Spirit to the church leaders to enact the consecration. We did not do what was asked at Fatima, and thus the consecration was made late in the century. As Sister Lucia once said, all of us failed in this regard. The Act of Consecration of Russia

---

[194] Matthew 24:22
[195] Ibid.
[196] "The Solar Miracle at Fatima", February 13, 2010. < www.virginmarywindow.com/the-solar-miracle-at-fatima >

started the period of peace promised by Blessed Mary at Fatima. She said once the consecration was enacted, a period of peace would be given to the world. And that period of peace is the apparition of Blessed Mary at Medjugorje. It is the period we are in now, a Period of Peace coexisting alongside Satan's time of Apostasy.

As foretold at Fatima, the Soviet Union spread her atheistic doctrine far beyond her borders, across Eastern Europe, China, Southeast Asia, Cuba, and even reaching some countries in Africa and a few regions of Central America. Everywhere communism was installed, Christianity was purposefully assailed. The USSR spread atheism by force of arms. In the time of the New Covenant, the Soviet Union fulfilled the role of the Roman legions and became the new abomination that caused the desolation and destruction of the holy people of God, this time not throughout only Judea and Jerusalem but throughout the world. While the Soviet system collapsed in 1991, its erroneous atheistic message lives on even now. That man is his own god is a prevalent idea in this time called the post-church era and of late called the time of neo-paganism. Just as the pagan empire of Rome surrounded and squeezed the holy people of Judea who worshipped the one true God, along with their holy city of Jerusalem, so now the holy peoples who adhere to the precepts of the Gospel (whether they be officially Christian or simply those who show love for neighbor and love for God) throughout the world are being oppressed. And as Rome was the governmental power, so too have the neo-pagans seized governmental power over the past thirty years, fostering their unholy and false teachings upon all, with the passage of unjust and intrinsically evil laws providing for abortion, and the removal of public reference to the one true God from the public square.

We are living in a time of a renewed message of atheism buttressed by the persecutions of the past century. One of the main points of attack by the atheists continues to be the question of the suffering of the innocents. While lacking the standing of Nietzsche and Marx, whose complicated arguments appealed primarily to the intelligentsia, the ideas of today's atheists such as Dawkins appeal to a wide audience. The earlier modernists undermined the foundations of the city of God, and then the persecutions led by the atheistic Russian nation destroyed much of that city, literally and figuratively, or, one should say, physically and spiritually. In the wake of the great tribulation Europe, the cradle of Christianity, has become a secularized society. Its beautiful churches are empty. Its people and their governments make decisions and laws without consideration being given to its foundational Judeo-Christian ethics.

"Have not we – the people of God – become to a large extent a people of unbelief and distance from God?" Pope Benedict asked at the 2011 Chrism in St. Peter's Basilica. In recognition of this apostasy, Pope Benedict XVI announced the creation of a new Vatican department called the Pontifical Council for the New Evangelization. It is aimed at bringing the Gospel back to Western societies that have lost their Christian identity, countries where the Gospel was first preached centuries ago, but where its presence in peoples' daily lives seems to be lost. Europe, the United States and Latin America are the focus of the new department.

Just as the disciples witnessed Judas betray Jesus towards the end of His days, we have witnessed priests betray the faith through the sexual abuse of minors.

Immediately after the tribulation of those days... the stars will fall from the sky, and the powers of the heavens will be shaken.[197]

From Daniel chapter 12, the word stars in this context means spiritual leaders such as bishops, priests, and presbyters, or devoted disciples of Christ:

But they that are learned [that is to say, learned in the law of God and true wisdom, which consists in knowing and loving God] *shall shine as the brightness of the firmament: and they that instruct many to justice, as stars for all eternity.*[198]

In our day we have seen many of our spiritual leaders fall.

The end of the Old Covenant is a type for the fulfillment of the New Covenant. But the fulfillment of the New Covenant will not lead to another covenant; rather it will mark the end of this present world. Sacred Scripture tells us the terrible Day of the Lord will come upon the world and the wicked will be burned away and seized and thrown into the fires of hell along with Satan and all of his demons. The New Covenant will be fulfilled. The world will be made anew, and will be inhabited by those who love God.

Jesus' passion, His bloody death at the end of the Old Covenant, is also a type that illustrates how the New Covenant will be fulfilled. In the

---

[197] Matthew 24:29
[198] Douay-Rheims Bible, Prophecy of Daniel Chapter 12:3, with parenthetical explanation of *learned*, from same source, added. May 31, 2010. < www.drbo.org/chapter/32012.htm>

twentieth century, even until today, the mystical Body of Christ is undergoing its passion, too. Christian peoples continue to "suffer on the cross" of atheistic and neo-pagan persecution, becoming martyrs as we approach the fulfillment of the New Covenant, which is the end of the present world. The death of Jesus, His blood sacrifice, opened the door to paradise. By the death and the blood and the sacrifice of the mystical Body of Jesus, the martyrs, most of whom were martyred in the middle of the twentieth century under atheistic communism, will pass through that open door of the cross and enter into paradise.

And then the sign of the Son of Man will appear in heaven, and all the tribes of the earth will mourn, and they will see the Son of Man coming upon the clouds of heaven with power and great glory.[199]

It is fitting then that the sub-period of the apostasy ends with the sign of the Son of Man in the sky. And the same sub-period of reconciliation at Medjugorje has for the pilgrims' penance the climb to the top of Cross Mountain. Just as Constantine's army, marked with the sign of the cross on their shields, triumphed over the persecution and apostasy of his time through the cross in the sky accompanied with the words, "in this sign, conquer", so too will our triumph come through the sign of the cross. In the 1930s, Jesus said to Saint Faustina:

Write this: before I come as the just Judge, I am coming first as the King of Mercy. Before the day of justice arrives, there will be given to people a sign in the heavens of this sort.

All light in the heavens will be extinguished, and there will be great darkness over the whole earth. Then the sign of the cross will be seen in the sky, and from the openings where the hands and the feet of the Savior were nailed will come forth great lights which will light up the earth for a period of time. This will take place shortly before the last day. (Diary, #83) [200]

---

[199] Matthew 24:30
[200] Faustina Maria Kowalska, *Diary of Saint Maria Faustina Kowalska: Divine Mercy in My Soul.* (Stockbridge, MA: Marian Press, 1987). ©1987 Marian Fathers of the Immaculate Conception. All rights reserved. Used with permission.

Chapter 15
The Great Tribulation

The period from the time of Fatima until the Act of Consecration of the world and Russia is the "times" of the beasts, the period of powerful, godless men who led the world to ruin. Jesus described it this way:

> *At that time there will be great tribulation, such as has not been since the beginning of the world until now, nor ever will be.*[201]

Russia, later the USSR, had been the most populous Christian nation, but became officially atheist virtually overnight in 1917. From that time until the final days of Soviet communism in 1991, millions of Christians were persecuted and killed. Archives released after the fall of communism in the USSR documented some of the horrors:

> November 1995: A Russian government commission issues a report stating that approximately 200,000 clerics in the Soviet Union were killed by the communists during the Soviet era. Describing some of the martyrdom, Alexander Yakolev, chairman of the commission, stated: "Clergymen and monks were crucified on the royal doors of churches, were shot dead, strangled, and had water poured on them in winter until they turned into frozen pillars."[202]

---

[201] Matthew 24:21
[202] Father Antonio Maria Martins, S.J., *Documents on Fatima & the Memoirs of Sister Lucia*. 2nd English ed. (Waite Park, MN: Park Press, 2002), 20. All rights reserved. Used with permission.

The Soviet Union was the first state to have and fully implement, as an ideological objective the elimination of religion. Toward that end, the Communist regime confiscated church property, ridiculed religion, harassed believers, and propagated atheism in the schools.[203]

The main target of the anti-religious campaign in the 1920s and 1930s was the Russian Orthodox Church, which had the largest number of faithful. Nearly all of its clergy, and many of its believers, were shot or sent to labor camps. Theological schools were closed and church publications were prohibited. By 1939 only about 500 of over 50,000 churches remained open.[204]

What happened in Vladivostok serves as an example for what happened to church communities throughout Russia. The Catholic population of 15,000 was killed outright, but there were too many Russian Orthodox. Two large, ornate Orthodox churches faced the main city square and were the gems of the city's faithful. In 1937, on Easter Sunday, these were dynamited into rubble. Other churches, including the Catholic Church edifice, were converted into government buildings. Parents were forbidden to teach religion to their children, enforced with an abhorrent punishment. Should a child mention something pertaining to religion to other children or adults, that child was taken away and not seen or heard from again. In this way, parents learned not to discuss religion in front of their children. The intent was to remove religion from the cultural memory in two generations.

At Fatima, Blessed Mary warned about Russia. In the First and Second World Wars, nation rose against nation. The Korean and Vietnam wars followed Word War II in quick succession, and there were many other wars throughout the century. In some of these wars, nations were annihilated, that is, they ceased to exist. Ukraine, Georgia, Latvia, Lithuania, and Belarus, among others, were absorbed into the Soviet Union and disappeared from the world map.

John Paul II is the pope most closely associated with Fatima because he was the target of an assassination attempt on the feast day of Our Lady of Fatima. He also made the act of consecration requested at Fatima in March 1984. He summarized the years of suffering of the 20th century when he said:

---

[203] "Revelations from the Russian Archives - Anti-Religious Campaigns", November 21, 2010.
<www.loc.gov/exhibits/archives/anti.html>
[204] Ibid.

How many victims there have been throughout the last century of the second millennium! We remember the horrors of the First and Second World Wars and the other wars in so many parts of the world, the concentration and extermination camps, the gulags, ethnic cleansings and persecutions, terrorism, kidnappings, drugs, the attacks on unborn life and the family.[205]

And Cardinal Ratzinger, now Pope Benedict XVI, in his commentary on the "Message of Fatima" in June 2000 spoke of the twentieth century, the century of Satan:

We can recognize the last century as a century of martyrs, a century of suffering and persecution for the Church, a century of World Wars and the many local wars which filled the last 50 years and have inflicted unprecedented forms of cruelty. Sr. Lucia wrote to the Holy Father on 12 May 1982: [author's note: about a year after the assassination attempt of 13 May 1981 on John Paul II] The Third Part of the Secret refers to Our Lady's words: "If not, [Russia] will spread her errors throughout the world, causing wars and persecutions of the Church. The good will be martyred; the Holy Father will have much to suffer; various nations will be annihilated."[206]

Famine was also mentioned at Fatima, and along with wars it too was prevalent throughout the twentieth century. An estimated seventy million people died from famine around the world. Some thirty million died during the famine of 1958–1961 in China. Other notable famines of the century include the 1942–1945 disaster in Bengal; famines in China in 1928 and 1942; and a sequence of famines in the Soviet Union, including the Holodomor, Stalin's famine inflicted on Ukraine in 1932–1933; the Biafran famine in the 1960s; and the disaster in Cambodia in the 1970s.[207] Pointedly, in the Olivet Discourse Jesus mentioned famine when He said, *"there will be famines and earthquakes from place to place."*[208]

---

[205] "The Holy Father's Beatification Homily", Oct. 21, 2010.
<http://www.ewtn.com/fatima/beatification/Homily.htm>
[206] Martins, *Documents on Fatima & the Memoirs of Sister Lucia,* 512. All rights reserved. Used with permission.
[207] Twentieth Century Atlas – Death Tolls, June 30, 2010. <http://necrometrics.com/20c5m.htm>
[208] USCCB-NAB-Matthew 24:7

Stalin's famine is particularly hideous, because it was orchestrated by the state:

> The dreadful famine that engulfed Ukraine, the northern Caucasus, and the lower Volga River area in 1932-1933 was the result of Joseph Stalin's policy of forced collectivization. The heaviest losses occurred in Ukraine, which had been the most productive agricultural area of the Soviet Union. Stalin was determined to crush all vestiges of Ukrainian nationalism.

> In 1932 Stalin raised Ukraine's grain buying quotas by forty-four percent. This meant there would not be enough grain to feed the peasants, since Soviet law required that no grain from a collective farm could be given to the members of the farm until the government's quota was met. Stalin's decision and the methods used to impose it condemned millions of peasants to death by starvation. Party officials, with the aid of regular troops and secret police units, waged a merciless war of attrition against peasants who refused to give up their grain. Even indispensable seed grain was forcibly confiscated from peasant households. Any man, woman, or child caught taking even a handful of grain from a collective farm could be, and often was, executed or deported. Those who did not appear to be starving were often suspected of hoarding grain. Peasants were prevented from leaving their villages by the NKVD and a system of internal passports.

> The death toll from the 1932-33 famine in Ukraine has been estimated between six million and seven million. According to a Soviet author, "Before they died, people often lost their senses and ceased to be human beings." Yet one of Stalin's lieutenants in Ukraine stated in 1933 that the famine was a great success.[209]

While it is difficult to get a handle on the sufferings of the twentieth century—there is just so much of it—Matthew White's website http://users.erols.com/mwhite28/atrox.htm tries to do just that. He coined a word for it, saying the twentieth century might come to be known as the *hemoclysm* (Greek for "blood flood") because this hemoclysm took the lives of some 155 million people. All in all, more than 80 percent of the deaths

---

[209] "Revelations from the Russian Archives – Ukrainian Famine", November 21, 2010. <www.loc.gov/exhibits/archives/anti.html>

caused by twentieth-century atrocities occurred in the hemoclysm (as opposed to naturally occurring deaths).[210]

No other period of human history comes close to this level of suffering, which brings us back to Matthew 24 and what Jesus said about the Great Tribulation: *"at that time there will be great tribulation, such as has not been since the beginning of the world until now, nor ever will be."* No other period of history has as much horror, cruelty and death as the major part of the twentieth century. In the past century, more people died of unnatural causes than in all other centuries, combined.

Fatima is undoubtedly the most prophetic of modern apparitions. The consecration of the world and Russia (re-named since 1917 as the USSR, but now once again called Russia) to the Immaculate Heart of Mary resulted in the end of the communist Soviet Union and the end of the spreading of Russia's error of atheism. It concludes a period of history marked by tragic human lust for power and evil. It concludes the "times" of the beasts.

The end of the Great Tribulation sub-period of the Short Time of Satan is not the end of the hundred years of Satan's extraordinary powers or his trials of the church. The Great Tribulation, the blood flood, came to an end and the barbarisms brought upon Christians in particular by the atheistic USSR ceased. The battle with the USSR climaxed on 13 May 1981 with the attempted assassination of Pope John Paul II, the representative of Christ on earth, in St. Peter's Square. But out of this supreme evil arose a supreme good. While recuperating, the pope read the official Church records of Fatima held in the Vatican archives and became determined to complete the consecration requested by Our Lady. It was precisely this consecration that saved us from nuclear war, a war in which millions would have died in an instant without time for repentance. Many souls would have been lost and atheistic communism might have spread throughout the world; as Jesus said, if not cut short, no one would have been saved.

---

[210] *Twentieth Century Atlas.* "Top Ranked Atrocities," March 15, 2010. <users.erols.com/mwhite28/atrox.htm>

Chapter 16
Shortened

Recall that Jesus said:

At that time there will be great tribulation, such as has not been since the beginning of the world until now, nor ever will be. And if those days had not been shortened, no one would be saved; but for the sake of the elect they will be shortened. [211]

At Fatima on 13 May 2000, at the Mass for the Beatification of Jacinta and Francisco, Pope John Paul II said:

Last Sunday at the Coliseum in Rome, we commemorated the many witnesses to the faith in the twentieth century, recalling the tribulations they suffered... Here in Fatima, where these times of tribulation were foretold and Our Lady asked for prayer and penance to shorten them, I would like today to thank heaven for the powerful witness shown in all those lives.[212]

Here he was alluding to the Fatima documents. While recuperating from his gunshot wounds suffered on 13 May 1981, noting the date of the attempted assassination he requested all of the documents on Fatima, including the third part of the secret. In those documents is a letter from

---

[211] USCCB-NAB-Matt. 24:21-22, June 3, 2010. <www.usccb.org/nab/bible/matthew/matthew24.htm>
[212] Beatification of Francisco and Jacinta Marto, March 8, 2010.
<www.vatican.va/holy_father/john_paul_ii/travels/documents/hf_jp-ii_hom_20000513_beatification-fatima_en.html>

Sister Lucia to Pius XII requesting the consecration of the world and Russia to the Immaculate Heart. That letter in part reads:

> I take this opportunity, Most Holy Father, to ask you to bless and extend this devotion [of the five first Saturdays] to the whole world. In 1929, through another apparition, our Lady asked for the consecration of Russia to Her Immaculate Heart, promising its conversion through this means and the hindering of the propagation of its errors.

> Sometime afterwards I told my confessor of the request of our Lady. He tried to fulfill it by making it known to Pius XI.

> In several intimate communications our Lord has not stopped insisting on this request, promising lately, to shorten the days of tribulation which He has determined to punish the nations for their crimes, through war, famine and several persecutions of the Holy Church and Your Holiness, if you will consecrate the world to the Immaculate Heart of Mary, with a special mention for Russia, and order that all the Bishops of the world do the same in union with Your Holiness.[213]

Our Lord shortened the Great Tribulation on 25 March 1984, the date of the consecration. The timeline correctly reflects this.

Satan's time should have ended at the close of the twentieth century, but apparently it extends past it by the same amount of time as from the consecration to the end of the century:

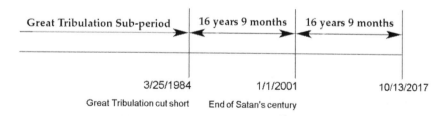

Jesus said the Great Tribulation which gets "cut short" would be followed immediately by the apostasy. And at Fatima Blessed Mary

---

promised a period of peace/reconciliation would follow the consecration, that is, after the act that shortened the Great Tribulation. This means the apostasy and the period of reconciliation occur simultaneously.

This requires reflection. Satan was granted not just time but also added power. His time and additional power were to last until the end of 31 December 2000 but this was cut short by sixteen years and nine months. Because Our Lady still warns us about Satan in her messages and she says his power over this world will end when the secrets she has confided to the visionaries begin to unfold, Satan is still at work. Our Lady appears daily. She gives monthly messages to the world that remind us to pray, to fast, and to convert. They are anti-Satan messages, and they have been given to the world since March of 1984. Beginning in 1984, Satan's added power to influence those who would do his bidding was countered by the influence of Blessed Mary to lead us from him. Because God granted Satan one hundred years and each day after the consecration was now split between Blessed Mary and himself, the remaining time in his century was doubled. He was given an additional sixteen years and nine months so that the total time remains the same. A graphical representation of this:

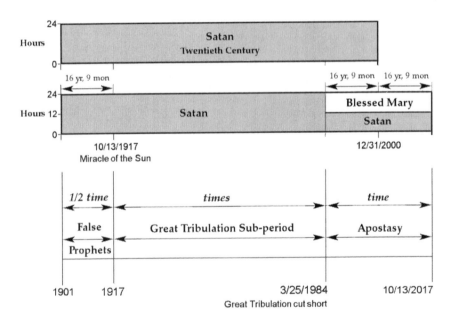

The shaded portion representing the time granted to Satan is the same in both graphs. God keeps His promises, even to Satan.

At Medjugorje on 25 January 1997, Blessed Mary said:

I invite you to reflect about your future. You are creating a new world without God... This time is my time and that is why...I invite you again to pray... I repeat to you that I am with you to help you.

From the unshaded portion of the graph it is apparent that Blessed Mary was referencing the "time" part of the latter days known also as the "time, times, and a half time" when she first used the word in her message (*This time...*). Our Lady thus indicates we are in that sub-period of the times of the end.

Near the very beginning of the Medjugorje apparitions on 2 August 1981 recall Blessed Mary said, "A great struggle is about to unfold, a struggle between my Son and Satan. Human souls are at stake."[214] This is illustrated by the second graph.

The entire twentieth century and the Age of the Church, and indeed the history of man from the time of Adam is one of battle between the forces of good and the powers of evil; the wheat and the tares. But Revelation's chapter 20 makes it clear the battle it is speaking of is the final battle that comes in the final Short Time of Satan after he is unchained and granted authority to act—after he is given added power for forty-two months—against the city of God. Forty-two months is another way of saying time, times and a half time; the Jewish year consisted of 360 days, so three and a half years is 1260 days or forty-two months.

The pope was shot on 13 May 1981, exactly 42 days before the first apparition of Our Lady at Medjugorje on 24 June 1981. This is another number that again connects our time to the time of the end:

From Revelation 13:

The beast was given a mouth uttering proud boasts and blasphemies, and it was given authority to act for forty-two months.[215]

From Blessed Mary at Medjugorje in 1999:

The hour has come when the demon is authorized to act with all his force and power. The present hour, is the hour of Satan.

---

[214] Rene Laurentin and R. Lejeune, *Messages and Teachings of Mary at Medjugorje.* (Milford, Ohio: The Riehle Foundation, 1988), 108.
[215] USCCB-NAB-Revelation 13:5, April 18, 2010.
<www.usccb.org/nab/bible/revelation/revelation13.htm>

Our Lady indicates we are in the final battle because she also says Satan's power in the world will be broken forever after the secrets unfold. From Revelation 20:

> They invaded the breadth of the earth and surrounded the camp of the holy ones and the beloved city... The Devil who had led them astray was thrown into the pool of fire and sulfur... will be tormented day and night forever and ever.

From Blessed Mary at Medjugorje in 1982:

> This century is under the power of the devil; but when the secrets confided to you come to pass, his power will be destroyed.[216]

The great struggle about to unfold is the final battle, called Armageddon:

> They then assembled the kings in the place that is named Armageddon.... He will go out to deceive the nations at the four corners of the earth, Gog and Magog, to gather them for battle; their number is like the sand of the sea. They invaded the breadth of the earth and surrounded the camp of the holy ones and the beloved city. But fire came down from heaven and consumed them.[217]

There have been the false prophets of modernism, and the physical persecutions for much of the twentieth century, and now the spiritual suffering from the anti-Christian errors spread from Russia to the rest of the world. And the catastrophic secrets of Medjugorje are still to come.

The surrounded camp of the holy ones and the beloved city is the great city Lucia saw in the period-of-peace vision. It is the community of people who worship God and try to remain faithful to His teachings. It is a great City of God that has been built across the world during the figurative one thousand years of the Church.

We are near the end of the century granted to Satan. For over a hundred years Satan and his followers have battered that great city, leaving it half in ruins. The Miracle of the Sun announced the arrival of atheistic Russia, Satan's blunt-force instrument. But the greatest miracle since the Apostles' time is more than a herald of the Great Tribulation. It is a typological preview of the fire of Revelation 20 that comes down from

---

[216] "Overview of Medjugorje", June 25, 2010. <www.medjugorje.org/overview.htm>
[217] USCCB-NAB-Revelation 16:16, 20:8-9, June 30, 2010.
<www.usccb.org/nab/bible/revelation/revelation20.htm>

heaven at the end of the final battle and consumes those razing the beloved city.

Bible verses are packed or layered with deep meanings, and in a similar way the apparitions are layered with deeper meanings. The final battle called Armageddon brings us back to Mount Carmel, to Elijah, to John the Baptist, and to the latest and last typological Elijah, Blessed Mary. *Har* means hill or mountain; thus we have *har-megiddo* (hill of Megiddo), or Armageddon. The plain of Megiddo lies to the east of Mount Carmel. Interestingly, Mary's hometown of Nazareth is further east and within sight of Mount Carmel. And several miles to the east of Nazareth is Mount Tabor rising up from the plain. Between the hills of Carmel and Tabor lies the plain of Megiddo, scene of the battle of Armageddon.

Looking east from Mount Carmel where Elijah called down the fire in the Old Testament, one sees Mount Tabor rising up from the plains. Mount Tabor is where Jesus was transfigured and Peter, James, and John saw Him in glory. The century's battle between Mary and Satan began when Our Lady called the fiery sun down from the heavens on the "Mount Carmel" of Fatima. It is raging now between the figurative hills of Carmel and Tabor at the place called Medjugorje, which means "between the hills." When the reign of Satan is broken at the end of the battle "between the hills" and the fire from heaven consumes him and his followers, will we be transfigured—changed in an instant—just as Christ was transfigured on Mount Tabor 2,000 years ago?

The last battle is not literally at Megiddo but instead it is the battle we are witnessing between the typological Elijah, Blessed Mary, rallying us with a daily powerful last call to conversion on the one side, and Satan and his allies who are heavily besieging the holy people of God on the other. These people of God are taking refuge in the great holy city behind the walls of the Gospel message of Jesus Christ. The people of Satan's camp over the past thirty years have climbed the towers of government and are now successfully usurping the laws of God—the Ten Commandments—on which society and government were built during the thousand year Age of the Church that flourished while Satan was bound. The antichrist is even now revealing himself in some of our laws that reflect the image of Satan instead of the image of God, such as those that permit abortion. Although half in ruins the great city that is the people of God will hold out long enough, "until the full number of the Gentiles comes in,"[218] since Jesus promised that it will stand even against the gates of hell.

---

[218] USCCB-NAB-Romans 11:25, May 10, 2010. <www.usccb.org/nab/bible/romans/romans11.htm>

Many holy saints down through the ages prophesied that in the latter times the role of Mary would be great. One of the most notable is St. Louis De Montfort (31 January 1673–28 April 1716), who wrote:

> But Mary's power over the evil spirits will especially shine forth in the latter times, when Satan will lie in wait for her heel, that is, for her humble servants and her poor children whom she will rouse to fight against him. In the eyes of the world they will be little and poor ... [but] in compensation for this they will be rich in God's graces, which will be abundantly bestowed on them by Mary ... They will be superior to all creatures by their great zeal and so strongly will they be supported by divine assistance that, in union with Mary, they will crush the head of Satan with their heel ... and bring victory to Jesus Christ.[219]

And also:

> The salvation of the world began through Mary and through her it must be accomplished. Mary scarcely appeared in the first coming of Jesus Christ so that men, as yet insufficiently instructed and enlightened concerning the person of her Son, might not wander from the truth by becoming too strongly attached to her. But in the second coming of Jesus Christ, Mary must be known and openly revealed by the Holy Spirit so that Jesus may be known, loved, and served through her ... God wishes ... to reveal Mary, his masterpiece, and make her more known in these latter times. As she was the way by which Jesus first came to us, she will again be the way by which he will come to us the second time though not in the same manner. In these latter times Mary must shine forth more than ever in mercy, power, and grace... to bring back and welcome lovingly the poor sinners and wanderers who are to be converted.[220]

Pope John Paul II was a follower of de Montfort and adopted his motto "*totus tuus,*" Latin for "totally yours," to express his strong devotion to Blessed Mary. John Paul said that reading de Montfort's True Devotion to the Blessed Virgin was a decisive turning point in his life.

---

[219] St. Louis de Montfort, *True Devotion to the Blessed Virgin.* Retrieved May 7, 2010. <www.montfort.org.uk/Writings/TrueDev.html> Used with Permission.
[220] Ibid.

Blessed Mary says, "The present hour, is the hour of Satan." But it is also the Age of Mary. And in the Age of Mary, the hour of Mary approaches. The triumph of her Immaculate Heart will be the fulfillment of her role in salvation history, when in these last days as the fire descends to consume us she intercedes and triumphs over our hearts and over evil and delivers through our conversion her offspring, the people of god, just as Esther intervened before the king to deliver her people from death and the day of their annihilation became the day of their triumph.

Queen Esther, a type for Blessed Mary of these times, asked her people to fast for her intentions, and Blessed Mary asks us to pray and fast now so that her intentions may be realized.

Dear children! Today again I am calling you to prayer and fasting. You know, dear children, that with your help I am able to accomplish everything...(4 September 1986)

I beseech all of you to offer prayers and sacrifices for my intentions so I can present them to God for what is most necessary. (25 September 1991)

Dear children! Sympathize with me! Pray, pray, pray! (Blessed Mary, 10 April 1984)

Jakov said: Our Lady spoke to me about the secrets and at the end said: *"Pray, pray, pray." (25 December 2010)*

In the battle to literally end all battles, the battle for our souls in these last times, we already know who wins. In the end my Immaculate Heart will triumph. Good will destroy evil, and we will live in the new heaven and new earth with Blessed Mary and the saints and God will dwell with us.

In this time of Mary, in the final hours of mankind's struggle, Our Lady tirelessly calls us as a mother calls her children. She asks us to be reconciled with God, to convert, and to decide for holiness so that she can help us by interceding for us before God:

Dear children! My prayer today is for all of you who seek the grace of conversion. You knock on the door of my heart, but without hope and prayer, in sin, and without the Sacrament of Reconciliation with God. Leave sin and decide, little children, for holiness. Only in this way can I help you, hear your prayers and seek intercession before the Most High. Thank you for having responded to my call. (25 May 2011)

Blessed Mary and her offspring will be victorious in the struggle with the powers of evil. Remember that her Immaculate Heart will triumph. But also remember Blessed Mary says this is the last time she will come to call us to conversion, so the time to convert is *now;* Unlike with Fatima, this time there is no "next time".

Chapter 17
The Vision of the Third Part of the Secret

Jesus told Lucia the consecration would be done but late, after the Soviet Union had already spread her errors in the world. In 1981 at Medjugorje, Blessed Mary said the Soviet Union would glorify God while the West had made civilization progress but without God, as if they were their own creators. Ironically, while Russia in 2010 has earmarked $150 million to renovate its churches and moves closer to once again reclaiming its place in history as one of the most Christian of nations, the West, contaminated by her (Soviet) errors, moves further away from God each year. The first nation to legalize abortion was the USSR in 1920.[221] The US legalized it in 1973, so clearly the world has become contaminated with the Soviet errors. And clearly the twentieth-century hemoclysm has subsided because of the Fatima consecration, but Satan's hundred years of extra power remain. The *"short time" of authority to act* granted to Satan as described in the Bible and foreseen by Pope Leo XIII did not end with the conclusion of the sub-period known as the Great Tribulation.

During the period of peace, which we are in now, what happens "next" has yet to be determined. One thing is certain: we are deep into the pages

---

[221] "The Democratic Argument in Soviet Debates Over the Legalization of Abortion in the 1920's", Susan Gross Soloman. February 13, 2010.<www.persee.fr/web/revues/home/prescript/article/cmr_0008-0160_1992_num_33_1_2306>

of Holy Scripture where Jesus gave His Olivet Discourse to His disciples, outlining the signs of His impending return.

The vision of the third part of the Secret of Fatima is a vision of the period of peace. It begins with an angel pointing with his right hand to the earth below and shouting "Penance, penance, penance." His left hand holds the instrument of that penance, a flaming sword from which emanates flames that appear to be about to consume the world. This calls to mind a passage from the New Testament that speaks of the final apostasy:

And then many will be led into sin; they will betray and hate one another. Many false prophets will arise and deceive many; and because of the increase of evildoing, the love of many will grow cold.[222]

The present heavens and earth have been reserved by the same word for fire, kept for the day of judgment...[223]

Here we are told that the world will face "fire" on the Day of Judgment. But note that in the Fatima vision the fire of judgment is blocked by the radiance of the Blessed Virgin Mary. On the earth below, we see the Pope making his way to the summit of a mountain where there is a large cross, followed by other religious and lay people. On his way, the Pope passes through a great city half in ruins. We now know it is John Paul II and the description in the third secret describes the Parkinson's-afflicted pope's latter years—walking "half trembling with halting step, afflicted with pain and sorrow." (In fact, in this physical predicament, he was asked why he didn't resign. He replied, "Because Jesus didn't come down off the cross,"[224] a statement that also implicitly acknowledges the pope's suffering was for us.)

Revelation's surrounded camp of the holy ones and the beloved city[225] is that great city half in ruins revealed to Lucia; it is St. Augustine's City of God. This people of God have been built up throughout the figurative one thousand years of teaching the Gospel throughout the world. For over a hundred years of added power Satan and those who follow him have

[222] USCCB-Matthew 24:10-12, March 6, 2010. <www.usccb.org/nab/bible/matthew/matthew24.htm>
[223] USCCB-NAB-2 Peter 3:3-4,7
[224] National Catholic Reporter. Obituary of Pope John Paul II, March 7, 2010.
<www.nationalcatholicreporter.org/update/conclave/jp_obit_main.htm#mystic>
[225] USCCB-NAB-Rev. 20:9, Nov. 14, 2010. <www.usccb.org/nab/bible/revelation/revelation20.htm>

attacked that city, battering it especially with the atheistic system introduced by revolutionary Russia. Under communism, the people of God suffered physical death through martyrdom. Under democracy, they suffered the spiritual death of apostasy through the spread of the errors of atheism and modernism.

Against this backdrop, in the third secret's vision the climax of the suffering comes when the pope and other religious and lay people are killed. In the fulfillment of that vision, the climax of Satan's century of attacks on the people of God comes in 1981 when Christ's head on earth is shot in an assassination attempt orchestrated by the USSR. "The twentieth century was one of the most crucial in human history, with its tragic and cruel events culminating in the assassination attempt on the [Pope]."[226]

This act of barbarism led to the Act of Consecration, which both ended the great tribulation sub-period and established the next sub-period of apostasy, which is also the sub-period of reconciliation between God and man (as explained in the previous section, "Shortened").

At Fatima, we were promised a period of peace and we have learned that by peace Our Lady was speaking of reconciliation. Medjugorje is that period of peace. On 26 June 1981, Blessed Mary said:

Peace, Peace, Peace! Be reconciled! Only Peace. Make your peace with God and among yourselves.

Then Our Lady proceeded in the same message to tell us how to make our peace with God, how we can be reconciled with Him:

For that, it is necessary to believe, to pray, to fast, and to go to confession.

And on 6 August 1981, the Virgin Mary said, "*I am the Queen of Peace.*"

As for the martyrs of the Church age, it is in the Fatima vision that we see the angels sprinkling the "souls making their way to God" with the blood of those martyrs. While this is happening, the splendor of the woman clothed with the sun restrains the flames of judgment aimed at the world.

---

[226] "The Message of Fatima," March 8, 2010.
<www.vatican.va/roman_curia/congregations/cfaith/documents/rc_con_cfaith_doc_20000626_message-fatima_en.html>

The blood of the martyrs shortened the Great Tribulation, "purchasing" for us this period of reconciliation before the last day.

> *I saw under the altar the souls of them that were slain for the word of God, and for the testimony which they held. And they cried with a loud voice, saying: How long, O Lord (holy and true) dost thou not judge and revenge our blood on them that dwell on the earth?*
> *And white robes were given to every one of them; and it was said to them, that they should rest for a little time, till their fellow servants, and their brethren, who are to be slain, even as they, should be filled up.*[227]

The mystic Saint Padre Pio once told Garabandal seer Conchita, "The great wonder of God [Miracle] must be paid for with much blood throughout Europe."[228] The blood of the martyrs along with our prayers and fasting will usher in the triumph of the Immaculate Heart of Mary, the time when many mystics have said the greatest number of souls will make their way to God. At Medjugorje on 26 June 1981 Our Lady said in response to a question on the purpose of her appearing there, *"I wish to convert all of you and to reconcile the whole world."*

Fatima's vision reveals the flaming sword about to set the world afire; its fiery descent of the sun previews the last day. In both of these we see the "fire came down from heaven and consumed them" of Revelation 20. At Medjugorje for the past thirty years conversions are slowly, inexorably taking place while the fire of judgment is restrained by the presence of Blessed Mary. Although half in ruins, the great city that is the people of God will hold out long enough, *"until the full number of the Gentiles comes in,"*[229] since Jesus promised that it will stand even against the gates of hell.

After the verses about apostasy in Matthew 24 cited above, Jesus said, *"But the one who perseveres to the end will be saved."* On 18 March 2008 Blessed Mary said, *"Be persevering so that, at the end of the way, we can all together, in joy and love, hold the hands of my Son. Come with me; fear not."*

In these latter days, with widespread abortion, rampant new-age beliefs and much more, we must remember that Blessed Mary prophesied at Fatima *"in the end, my Immaculate Heart will triumph."* Blessed Mary and her

[227] Douay-Rheims Bible, Revelation 6:9-11, Nov. 14, 2010. <www.drbo.org/chapter/ 73006.htm>
[228] Garabandal's Prophecy About Communism, January 6, 2011.
<www.ourlady.ca/info/communism.htm>
[229] USCCB-NAB-Romans 11:25

offspring will be victorious over the powers of evil. On 2 June 2007, Our Lady said to Mirjana:

Dear children! Also in this difficult time God's love sends me to you. My children, do not be afraid, I am with you! With complete trust give me your hearts, that I may help you to recognize the signs of the time in which you live. I will help you to come to know the love of my Son. I will triumph through you. Thank you.

Summarizing:

- The Act of Consecration on 25 March 1984 cut short the Great Tribulation.
- The period of peace is more properly called the period of reconciliation between God and man.
- This period was promised at Fatima to follow the "times" sub-period where beasts, godless men, destroyed a large part of the symbolic city of God—"a great city half in ruins".
- This period occurs simultaneously with the Apostasy, the final falling away from the faith. Rather than letting mankind, so broken and battered by the Great Tribulation, lose all hope and fall away to the Evil one, God sent Blessed Mary as a soothing medicine to the nations to nurture us back to Him at this time.
- The blood of the martyrs of the Great Tribulation is used by God to help those who come afterwards to reconcile, to make their peace with God, to get up from their fallen, shattered lives and climb back to Him. Prayers and sacrifices such as fasting by the people are also used by God for our reconciliation.
- The flaming sword that will set the world afire is being held back while Our Lady is here, giving all of us time to return to God should we so choose. Indications are once this time is fulfilled, the present world will be consumed by the flames of the sword of the angel, as foreshadowed by the Miracle of the Sun.

Chapter 18
Simchat Torah

The Hebrew word for feasts (moadim) literally means "appointed times." It is God Who appoints them. We have already encountered this word in the expression "the time, times, and a half time". More literally it is "the appointed time, and the appointed times, and the appointed half a time", which restores its gravitas.

Because its root is moadim, a better translation of the Hebrew of Genesis 1:14 replaces the word seasons with festivals:

And God said: Let there be lights made in the firmament of heaven, to divide the day and the night, and let them be for signs, and for [festivals], and for days and years[230]

God appointed the feasts of Israel, and the moon determines their timing:

And the moon in all in her seasons, is for a declaration of times and a sign of the world. From the moon is the sign of the festival day... By the words of the holy one [the sun and the moon] shall stand in judgment, and shall never fail in their watches.[231]

For example, in ancient times the beginning of Passover was determined by the first full moon after the spring equinox.

---

[230] Douay-Rheims Bible, Book of Genesis 1:14, May 31, 2010. <www.drbo.org/chapter/01001.htm>
[231] Douay-Rheims Bible, Ecclesiasticus 43:6-7,11

Throughout our ketubah, the Holy Scriptures, God provides information about His plan for our salvation. An important part of this is the Jewish feasts, both the appointed feasts and the rabbinical feasts. Each provides a type for the salvific work of His Messiah. In Leviticus 23, God gives the appointed time of the seven Feasts of the Lord celebrated throughout the year. The seven feasts are split across two seasons, the spring and the fall, corresponding to the two agricultural seasons in Israel. There is a time of rain in the spring (early rain) and a time of rain in the fall (latter rain). These relate to the two comings of the Messiah as revealed in Scripture:

> *He will revive us after two days: on the third day he will raise us up, and we shall live in his sight...His going forth is prepared as the morning light, and he will come to us as the early and the latter rain to the earth.*[232]

At the end of the spring rain came the grain harvest and at the end of the autumn season, the fruit harvest. We see typology here—at the Passover meal the bread (from grain) and wine (fruit of the vine) became the body and blood of Jesus the Messiah.

Between the two rains there is a long hot summer in Israel. Again typologically, this corresponds to the time of the Gentiles, the time between the two comings of Christ.

God has carefully planned the timing and sequence of each of His appointed feasts to reveal to us the two comings of His Messiah. Also, God inspires the rabbinical feasts and so they too have an important role in the story of our salvation. The four spring feasts are: Passover, the Feast of Unleavened Bread, the Feast of Firstfruits, and the Feast of Shavuot, also known as Pentecost. Coming almost two months after Passover, Pentecost is near the beginning of the long hot summer. After the Jews received the Torah at Mount Sinai on the Feast of Shavuot, they wandered forty long years in the dry desert before reaching the Promised Land; typologically after these "days of summer", the autumn feasts will announce the return of the Messiah and our entry into the promised land of Heaven.

Passover foreshadows the Messiah as our Passover lamb whose blood is shed for our sins. Jesus was crucified on the day of preparation at the same hour that the lambs were being slaughtered for the Passover meal that evening.

---

[232] Douay-Rheims Bible, Hosea 6:3

Unleavened Bread foreshadows the Messiah's life without sin (leaven is symbolically associated with sin in the Bible). Jesus' body, the perfect unblemished sacrificial lamb, was in the tomb during this feast. The body of Christ is unleavened bread; He is sinless.

Firstfruits foreshadows the Messiah's resurrection as the first fruit of the harvest. Jesus rose from the dead on this day as Saint Paul tells us when he refers to Jesus as the first fruits:

> *But now Christ has been raised from the dead, the first fruits of those who have fallen asleep. For since death came through a human being, the resurrection of the dead came also through a human being. For just as in Adam all die, so too in Christ shall all be brought to life, but each one in proper order: Christ the first fruits; then, at his coming, those who belong to Christ.*[233]

The Lord told Moses that on this day the people shall bring the first of the spring harvest and the priest shall wave it before the Lord to symbolize dedicating it to Him, "so that you may be accepted." Jesus' resurrection was like a wave offering presented to the Father as the first fruits of the harvest to come, at the end of the age.

Pentecost is both the feast when God created the covenant with Israel and centuries later, the renewed covenant with the Church. Moses gave the Israelites the ten commandments of the covenant written in stone; the Holy Spirit gave to the Church God's laws written on our hearts.

Jesus in the New Testament has already fulfilled the springtime feasts. In ancient Israel, in the summer preparations were made for the fall harvest and its feasts. Typologically we are in the summer and the spreading of the teachings of Jesus and the enlarging of the Kingdom of God are the preparations for the second Coming at the end of the autumn harvest. After Pentecost four months pass before the first of the fall feasts, the Feast of Trumpets. This prefigures the patient wait of the Church for the return of Christ, the symbolic thousand years of Revelation 20.

The appointed feasts of the latter rains are Trumpets, the Day of Atonement, and Tabernacles. The day after Tabernacles is the rabbinical feast of Shemini Atzeret. And the day after that is the last of the annual feasts, Simchat Torah. (For the Diaspora it is the day after Shemini Atzeret;

---

[233] USCCB-NAB-1 Corinthians 15:20-23, April 15, 2010.
<www.usccb.org/nab/bible/1corinthians/1corinthians15.htm>

for Jews living in Israel, Shemini Atzeret and Simchat Torah are celebrated on the same day.) The fall feasts occur within a short twenty-three-day period so once the days marking His return begin, Jesus will come quickly.

The Feast of Trumpets marks the beginning of a ten-day period of prayer, self-examination and repentance that culminates on Yom Kippur, the Day of Atonement. The Feast of Trumpets is also known as the Day of Remembrance because of the commandment to remember to blow the trumpet called the shofar, to crown God as King of the Universe. The sound of the trumpet is meant to jolt us from our sleep. We are to remember that we are God's people and that He is our King. The trumpet will alert Jews and Christians to repent because the King is approaching. When the bridegroom returned after preparing a place in his father's house and approached the village of the bride, a horn and shouting would ring out to alert the bride and her relatives he was nearby and would be there soon.

In Jewish custom, on this day the righteous are written in the Book of Life and the wicked are written in the Book of Death. However, many are not inscribed in either book but have until Yom Kippur to repent before sealing their fate. Thus the greeting given at this time: May you be inscribed and sealed for a good year. The ten days between Trumpets and Yom Kippur are the Days of Repentance. During the ten days one can change the outcome by repentance, prayer, and good works (usually works of charity are performed at this time), and it is common to seek reconciliation with those you may have wronged during the past year. The "books" are sealed on Yom Kippur, the Day of Atonement.

The Day of Atonement is a day set aside to "afflict the soul," to atone for the sins of the past year. On Yom Kippur the judgment entered in the book of life or the book of death is sealed. This day is the last appeal, the last chance to change the judgment through repentance. This is the holiest day on the Jewish calendar. Even non-observant Jews do not work, fast, and attend synagogue on this day. After Yom Kippur comes the Feast of Sukkot.

Sukkot commemorates the forty-year period during which the chosen people of Israel were wandering in the desert, living in temporary shelter. Sukkot is a harvest festival and is sometimes called the Festival of Ingathering. From the Christian perspective this will come around the time of the Messiah's return, and will signify the final harvest of the wheat and the weeds—the weeds will be gathered up from the wheat and thrown into the fire and burned. The wheat—those who love God by following His commandments—will remain and Jesus will dwell with them forever.

Sukkot became the most important feast in Judaism, as indicated by its designation as "the Feast of the Lord" or simply "the Feast". The seventh day of Sukkot is known as Hoshana Rabbah, or Great Supplication, and it is marked by seven processions where the worshippers ask God, "Please save us." The last hymn of the procession is unique and it starts and ends with "The voice of the herald heralds and says." The herald is Elijah, and the hymn anticipates the coming of the Messiah. It is customary for the scrolls of the Torah to be removed from the ark during this procession. Again the typology is apparent here—Jesus is the True Torah, and the ark holding the scrolls is Blessed Mary. Jesus came to us through Mary and Jesus is expected to return to us through Mary, although in a different way the second time. On this last day of the harvest feast, the people call upon the Lord to save them which is figurative of how the people will implore the Messiah to save them when He comes on the Last Day. In addition, jubilee years are proclaimed during the Feast of Sukkot. The Messiah is expected to come in a jubilee year, and He is expected to proclaim the jubilee by bringing glad tidings to the lowly, healing the brokenhearted, proclaiming liberty to the captives and release to the prisoners, announcing both a year of favor and a day of vengeance by God, while comforting all who mourn. In other words, the Feast of the Lord heralds His coming and the time of salvation for His people. Hoshana Rabbah is known as the last of the Days of Judgment, which began on the Feast of Trumpets.

Harvest is a common biblical metaphor for the time of God's judgment. In Joel we read:

> *For there I will sit in judgment upon all the neighboring nations. Apply the sickle, for the harvest is ripe.*[234]

And in the Gospel of Matthew, we find the well-known parable of the sower and the harvest:

> *The kingdom of heaven may be likened to a man who sowed good seed in his field. While everyone was asleep his enemy came and sowed weeds all through the wheat...at harvest time I will say to the harvesters, 'First collect the weeds and tie them in bundles for burning; but gather the wheat into my barn.'*[235]

---

[234] USCCB-NAB-Joel 4:12-13, November 27, 2010. <www.usccb.org/nab/bible/joel/joel4.htm>
[235] USCCB-NAB-Matt. 13:24-30, Nov.27, 2010. <www.usccb.org/nab/bible/matthew/matthew13.htm>

The Zohar[236] says that while the judgment for the new year is sealed on Yom Kippur, it is not "delivered" until the last day of Sukkot. Until then, each individual verdict and decree for the New Year can be altered, so the blessing that Jews give to each other on the last day of Sukkot, in English "A good note", is a wish that the verdict will be positive. This reminds us of the Christian belief that while still alive it is never too late to repent and return to God and be forgiven.

Sukkot lasts for seven days. The two days following the festival, Shemini Atzeret and Simchat Torah, are separate holidays but are related to Sukkot. Although not technically correct, they are commonly thought of as a part of Sukkot.

In Israel, Shemini Atzeret is also the holiday of Simchat Torah. Outside of Israel—the Diaspora—only the second day of Shemini Atzeret is Simchat Torah, so Shemini Atzeret is Tishri 22 and 23, and Simchat Torah is Tishri 23. Shemini Atzeret literally means "the assembly of the eighth", meaning the eighth day, the day after the seventh day of Sukkot. One explanation for it is that Sukkot, the Feast of the Ingathering, is for all mankind, while Shemini Atzeret is for the people of God. The last day of Sukkot is one of judgment, when the weeds are thrown into the fire. The next day, the eighth, the "wheat" are assembled before God, Who dwells with them. The Rejoicing in the Torah, the feast of Simchat Torah, follows this.

Simchat Torah is the last festival of God in His calendar year, and so it is called the Last Great Day. Simchat Torah, the Jewish feast day of "Rejoicing in the Torah," marks the completion of the annual cycle of weekly Torah readings. Each week in synagogue, a portion of the Torah is read. The annual cycle covers the Torah from the first portion of Genesis 1 to the last portion, Deuteronomy 34. On Simchat Torah, the last Torah portion is read, and the reading for that day proceeds to the first chapter of Genesis, reminding the Jewish people that the Torah is a never-ending circle.

This completion of the Torah readings is a time of great celebration for the Jews. There are processions around the synagogue carrying

---

[236] The Zohar is the foundational work in the literature of Jewish mystical thought. It is a group of books that covers the mystical aspects of the Torah.

Torah scrolls and plenty of high-spirited singing and dancing in the synagogue with the Torahs ... As many people as possible are given the honor of an aliyah (reciting a blessing over the Torah reading); in fact, even children are called for an aliyah blessing on Simchat Torah. In addition, as many people as possible are given the honor of carrying a Torah scroll in these processions. Children ... often follow the procession around the synagogue, sometimes carrying small toy Torahs.[237]

The Jews rejoice in the Torah, and God rejoices in His Torah being with the Jewish people, His chosen.

The three holidays of Sukkot, Shemini Atzeret, and Simchat Torah are similar in certain respects to the week of a Jewish wedding. Sukkot is like a golden week of pre-wedding celebrations, involving many people. On Shemini Atzeret, it becomes more intimate and involves the immediate family.

Much of the symbolism of Simchat Torah is that of a wedding ceremony. The special title given to the honorees called for the last aliyah in Deuteronomy and the first aliyah in Genesis—Hattan (groom) / Kallat (bride) Torah and Hattan / Kallat Breishit, respectively—remind us of this. Similarly, particularly for these aliyot, it is customary to read the Torah under a huppah, or wedding canopy. In a larger sense, the food, song and dance help us to celebrate the marriage between God and the Jewish people. The Torah is the ultimate ketubah or wedding contract.[238]

Sometimes at an Orthodox Jewish celebration of Simchat Torah rice is joyously thrown at the Torah scrolls as a reminder that each Jewish person is married to the Torah.

For Christians the Jewish wedding and its customs present a type for the covenant between Christ the groom, considered the True Torah by Christians, and His bride the Church. So it is fitting on Simchat Torah, the Last Great Day and a type for the Last Day much of the symbolism and celebration is that of a wedding feast.

---

[237] "Judaism 101: Shemini Atzeret and Simchat Torah." March 29, 2010. <www.jewfaq.org/holiday6.htm>
[238] "Dancing with Scrolls!" April 26, 2011. <www.uscj.org/Simchat_Torah5657.html>

On 13 October 2017, the one-hundredth anniversary of the Miracle of the Sun, Jewish people around the world will celebrate Simchat Torah — the Last Great Day. In Deuteronomy 34 Moses completes his task of leading God's people to the Promised Land, and then, in Genesis 1, God creates the heavens and the earth. It is interesting that 13 October 2017 falls on the Feast of the Last Great Day because it is the last day of our timeline that we created from an analysis of time, times and a half time of Daniel's time of the end. Is this the long awaited day of the triumph of the Immaculate Heart of Mary, or of something more? Is it possible that on 13 October 2017 man's journey through the desert to the Promised Land could reach its destination of the promised land of Deuteronomy 34, followed by the new heaven and new earth in both Genesis and the book of Revelation? Was this the day prefigured by the sun miracle, the day when the purifying fire of the Holy Spirit descends and generates the new heaven and a new earth? Does this Jewish feast prefigure the Day of the Lord that results in great rejoicing in the True Torah, in rejoicing in Jesus Who is the Word of God being with His people?

We cannot know the answers to these questions. But we can say this with certainty: With the Miracle of the Sun and the typology of the triumph of Queen Esther on the thirteenth of the month, God has underlined 13 October 2017 in bold strokes. The day 13 October 2017 is a key date in salvation history.

Chapter 19
The Permanent Sign

By the blood of the lamb on the doorposts the Hebrews were delivered out of Egypt and into the desert to the foot of Mount Sinai. But the people were not yet God's chosen. Assembled before Mount Sinai, they waited while Moses went up the mountain and brought the covenant down to them, a covenant that said if they remained faithful to God by obeying His commands they would be His people and He would be their God and protect them and deliver them as He had delivered them out of Egypt "on eagle wings":

> ...after their departure from the land of Egypt... the Israelites came to the desert of Sinai... While Israel was encamped here in front of the mountain, Moses went up the mountain to God. Then the LORD called to him and said, "Thus shall you say to the house of Jacob; tell the Israelites: You have seen for yourselves...how I bore you up on eagle wings and brought you here to myself. Therefore, if you hearken to my voice and keep my covenant, you shall be my special possession, dearer to me than all other people, though all the earth is mine. You shall be to me a kingdom of priests, a holy nation. That is what you must tell the Israelites." So Moses went and summoned the elders...When he set before them all that the LORD had ordered him to tell them, the people all answered together, "Everything the LORD has said, we will do."[239]

---

[239] USCCB-NAB-Exodus 19:1-8, April 13, 2010. <www.usccb.org/nab/bible/exodus/exodus19.htm>

God proposed marriage to the people of Israel, becoming a husband to them. In a traditional Jewish wedding the bride goes through a ritual washing called a Mikvah before meeting her bridegroom. The passage of the Israelites through the Red Sea was the Mikvah cleansing of the bride Israel before the wedding. Next the bride and groom meet under the Chuppah which to this day is usually outdoors, to form the covenant of marriage; the Israelites met their Groom under the heights of Mount Sinai. The Hebrew wedding is sealed with the ketubah, the marriage contract that lists the rights and duties of the parties joining in the marriage covenant. Moses brought to the people the proposal from God, the Torah, the ketubah. To this day in the traditional Jewish wedding the ketubah is read aloud. After Moses read the Torah aloud to the people, the people accepted the proposal, becoming the bride of God, and Moses sprinkled the altar and the assembled people with the blood of the covenant:

> *Moses then wrote down all the words of the LORD...Moses took half of the blood and put it in large bowls; the other half he splashed on the altar. Taking the book of the covenant, he read it aloud to the people, who answered, "All that the LORD has said, we will heed and do." Then he took the blood and sprinkled it on the people, saying, "This is the blood of the covenant which the LORD has made with you in accordance with all these words of his."* [240]

From there they began the journey to the Promised Land. The Israelites spent forty years in the desert nourished with the bread called manna. At the end of that journey they arrived at the river Jordan, swollen with the harvest rains. God ordered Joshua to tell the people the night before the crossing to prepare by sanctifying themselves:

> *And Joshua said to the people: "Be sanctified. For tomorrow the Lord will accomplish miracles among you."* [241]

The Lord told Joshua to have the priests carry the Ark of the Covenant on their shoulders into the swollen Jordan. The moment they entered the river it stopped flowing and backed up all the way to a place called Adam:

> *The people struck their tents to cross the Jordan, with the priests carrying the ark of the covenant ahead of them. No sooner had these priestly bearers of the*

---

[240] Exodus 24:4,6-8
[241] USCCB-NAB-Joshua 3:5, April 14, 2010. <www.usccb.org/nab/bible/joshua/joshua3.htm>

ark waded into the waters at the edge of the Jordan, which overflows all its banks during the entire season of the harvest, than the waters flowing from upstream halted, backing up in a solid mass for a very great distance indeed, from Adam...while those flowing downstream toward the Salt Sea of the Arabah disappeared entirely...While all Israel crossed over on dry ground, the priests carrying the ark of the covenant...remained motionless on dry ground in the bed of the Jordan until the whole nation had completed the passage.[242]

At God's command, Joshua had a permanent sign placed at the location in the river where the priests had stood with the ark:

Joshua said to them: "Go to the bed of the Jordan in front of the ark...lift to your shoulders one stone apiece... In the future, these are to be a sign among you. When your children ask you what these stones mean to you, you shall answer them, 'The waters of the Jordan ceased to flow before the ark of the covenant of the LORD when it crossed the Jordan.' Thus these stones are to serve as a perpetual memorial to the Israelites." ... Joshua also had twelve stones set up in the bed of the Jordan on the spot where the priests stood who were carrying the ark of the covenant. They are there to this day.[243]

In summary, God bore the people of Israel out of Egypt "on eagle wings" into the desert and gathered them at Mount Sinai. He became their bridegroom by establishing His covenant with them, a covenant sealed in sacrificial blood. After this, the journey across the desert began. For forty years the chosen people wandered in the desert led by the ark and nourished with daily manna. Those who did not persevere in the faith died in that wilderness. The faithful reached the river Jordan and gazed across its swollen banks into the Promised Land. Then, led by the ark which stopped the flow of the river they crossed over to the Promised Land. God ordered a permanent sign to mark the place of the crossing. That is the story of the covenant between God and His chosen people the Hebrews, what Christians call the Old Covenant.

The establishment of the Old Covenant is a type for the creation of the New. The crossing of the Red Sea is a type for our baptism. Moses is a type for Jesus. Moses delivers the people of God out of Egypt, a type for this world of mammon. Jesus delivers the people of God—all of us—out of

---

[242] Joshua 3:13-17
[243] Joshua 4:4-9

bondage to sin and its wage, death. The blood of the lamb on the doorposts prefigures the blood of Christ, the Lamb of God, on the cross. Moses sprinkled the blood of the sacrifice on the altar and the people. Jesus' sacrificial blood flowed on Calvary, the sacrificial altar of God and at the last Supper, He offered the cup of the blood of the New Covenant to His disciples, His Church, His people. The cup held wine that He changed into His blood. That offered cup is the marriage proposal of the New Covenant. At Sinai, the people agreed to be faithful to God and Moses sprinkled both the altar and the people with the blood of the covenant, and the people became the bride of God; when we drink from the cup, we agree to the new covenant and become the bride of Christ; we say yes to our groom. We accept the New Covenant. The Israelites began their desert journey after making the covenant, and likewise the people of God—the Church—begin their desert journey across the wilderness after entering into covenant with the Lord in Baptism and Holy Eucharist. The forty years in the wilderness after entering into Covenant is a type for our journey in faith. It takes forty weeks for a pregnancy; the forty years are a type for each of us to become a new person, to be born again. The Israelites were given daily manna, the bread from heaven, to sustain them; we are given the daily Eucharist, the true bread come down from heaven. Those Israelites who persevered in the faith reached the Promised Land. If we persevere in the faith we will reach heaven—the one who perseveres to the end will be saved (Matt 24:13). In the old covenant the laws of God were written in stone; in the new covenant God writes His laws on our hearts. Our God is a consuming fire, and when we eat the true manna come down from heaven we are inwardly transformed. Moses presented the Torah, the ketubah, on Shavuot also called Pentecost, and on the Feast of Pentecost the Holy Spirit descended and consumed and changed in an instant all of the members of the nascent Church and tongues of fire appeared upon them. They became filled with all truth and love of God—they became united to God in the family of God,.

Historically we know when the tribal group called the Israelites, the chosen people of God, crossed the river and entered the Promised Land. Each of us in the New Covenant is personally journeying throughout our lives towards heaven. But our wedding contract, the Holy Scriptures, also indicates that the corporate body of the people of God is on a journey to the fulfillment of the New Covenant when the earth is restored to its original glory. The journey began at the time of Jesus. On this journey the teachings of Jesus are spread across the globe to all peoples. When that is completed the corporate city of God will cross over into the promised land of heaven. But before that happens, Sacred Scripture warns us that Satan will be released for a time, times and a half time, and he will try to destroy God's people.

From Sacred Scripture and private revelations of these times, can we learn anything about the crossing of the river by the corporate city of God that happens at the end of the age? The answer is yes. Some of the elements purposefully mentioned in the story of Israel's exodus are:

- the burning bush
- the eagle
- the sprinkling of sacrificial blood of the covenant on the altar and the people, marking the covenant between God and Israel
- nourishment in the desert
- a swollen river at the time of the harvest
- sanctification before crossing the river
- the ark borne by priests blocks the river back to Adam, thus allowing God's people to cross
- a permanent sign at the spot where the ark was held by the priests in the river during the crossing.

In Revelation 12 we find the eagle, nourishment in the desert, and a swollen river:

And a great sign appeared in heaven: A woman clothed with the sun, and the moon under her feet, and on her head a crown of twelve stars: And being with child, she cried travailing in birth, and was in pain to be delivered...And she brought forth a man child, who was to rule all nations with an iron rod: and her son was taken up to God, and to his throne...And there were given to the woman two wings of a great eagle, that she might fly into the desert unto her place, where she is nourished for a time and times, and half a time, from the face of the serpent. And the serpent cast out of his mouth after the woman, water as it were a river; that he might cause her to be carried away by the river. And the earth helped the woman, and the earth opened her mouth, and swallowed up the river, which the dragon cast out of his mouth. And the dragon was angry against the woman: and went to make war with the rest of her seed, who keep the commandments of God, and have the testimony of Jesus Christ. [244]

---

[244] Douay-Rheims Bible, The Apocalypse Of Saint John Chapter 12:1-2,5,14-17, June 3, 2010.
<www.drbo.org/chapter/73012.htm>

In particular, the eagle connects this passage to the exodus story. God told Moses He bore the people up on eagle wings and brought them into the desert to Himself, nourishing them with manna.

The woman in the passage is a complex symbol. We know she represents Christians and the Church, the people of the New Covenant, because it says her seed are those who follow the teachings of Jesus. But she is also Blessed Mary because she gives birth to a man who will rule all nations, and that is Jesus. The woman symbol has at least two meanings, so the passage can be interpreted in at least two different ways.

As for the meaning of the river cast out of the mouth of the serpent, Pope Benedict XVI recently provided what he called one of many beautiful interpretations:

> I think that the river is easily interpreted: these are the currents that dominate all and wish to make faith in the Church disappear, the Church that seems no longer to have a place in the face of the force of these currents [here he is referring to what he said earlier—mammon, terroristic ideologies, drugs, modernism] that impose themselves as the only rationality, as the only way to live. And the earth that absorbs these currents is the faith of the simple people, that does not allow itself to be overcome by these rivers and that saves the Mother and saves the Son.... This true wisdom of simple faith, that does not allow itself to be swamped by the waters, is the force of the Church.[245]

In the passage we are told the timeframe when the people cross the river by the words time, times, and a half time. This is the same time given in Daniel to indicate the length of the time of the end: how long will it be before all these things are finished? It will be for a time, times and a half time. This is the time granted to Satan, but here we see it is also the time given to the woman, Mary, the mother of the Church.

At Fatima Lucia said Our Lady was clothed with the sun, as in the verses above. And at Medjugorje the seers say Blessed Mary appears with a crown of twelve stars, again as in the verses above. So Blessed Mary reveals herself to us in the apparitions as this woman of Revelation. And the timing of the events of Fatima reveals the time, times and a half time of Revelation.

---

[245] Meditation of His Holiness Benedict XVI During the First General Congregation, November 21, 2010. <www.vatican.va/holy_father/benedict_xvi/speeches/2010/october/documents/hf_ben-xvi_spe_20101011_meditazione_en.html>

The woman gives birth in pain because Jesus is the Church, and the mystical body of Christ that is the Church was born in the blood of the cross and grows through the blood of the martyrs. It is the process of the transformation of the world, which costs blood, costs the suffering of the witnesses to Christ.[246]

The labor pains take us back once again to the Olivet Discourse where Jesus said this about the tribulations of the end times: All these are the beginning of the labor pains (Matt 24:8).

Through all the generations, Christ gathers humanity into himself in His passion of the cross. And the blood of the martyrs in the Age of the Church belongs to His passion. Lucia saw this in the vision of two angels below the arms of the cross sprinkling the blood of the martyrs on the souls making their way to God as they climbed a mountain to the cross. The cross at the top of the mountain symbolizes the altar of God. The sprinkling of the sacrificial blood of the martyrs on the people connects the Fatima vision with the blood of the covenant of Mount Sinai where Moses sprinkled the blood of the covenant on the altar and on the people after their deliverance from bondage in Egypt; and it connects it with the blood of the New Covenant of the cross on Calvary, and of the Mass.

At the beginning of his mission to deliver God's people from bondage, a burning bush that did not consume anything appeared, and Moses was sent to lead God's people out of Egypt. This is a type for Our Lady's mission. At the beginning of Blessed Mary's appearance at Medjugorje, the people saw a burning bush that did not consume anything. And Blessed Mary has told us God sent her to lead us to salvation.

> There an angel of the LORD appeared to him in fire flaming out of a bush. As he looked on, he was surprised to see that the bush, though on fire, was not consumed... I have come down to rescue them from the hands of the Egyptians and lead them out of that land into... a land flowing with milk and honey.[247]

At Medjugorje on 28 October 1981 several hundred people saw, at the site of the first apparition, a fire that burned without burning anything, and that evening Our Lady told the seers:

---

[246] Ibid.
[247] USCCB-NAB-Exodus 3:2,8,17, April 15 2010. <www.usccb.org/nab/bible/exodus/exodus3.htm>

The fire seen by the faithful was of a supernatural character. It is one of the signs, a forerunner of the great sign.

Revelation 12 says the earth helped the woman and opened its mouth and swallowed the flood spewed out of the dragon's mouth. Above, Pope Benedict explains the earth is the simple people of faith who reside in the Church. At Fatima and Medjugorje Blessed Mary repeatedly calls us to open our mouths in prayer and to spread her messages and to witness our Christian vocation in order to help her.

On 27 September 1984:
Your prayers are helping my plans to be fulfilled. Pray continually for their complete fulfillment. I beg the families of the parish to pray the family rosary.

On 25 November 2004:
At this time, I call you all to pray for my intentions. Especially, little children, pray for those who have not yet come to know the love of God and do not seek God the Savior. You, little children, be my extended hands and by your example draw them closer to my Heart and the Heart of my Son.

From Blessed Mary's message to the world, 25 March 2010:
Also today I desire to call you all to be strong in prayer and in the moments when trials attack you. Live your Christian vocation in joy and humility and witness to everyone.

And there are many more messages from Blessed Mary that call us to pray, to witness to the Gospel, and to spread her messages.

The Ark of the Covenant led the people of God across the desert and across the swollen river into the Promised Land. Mary the Ark of the New Covenant is leading her children, the people of God, across the swollen river of neo-paganism, modernism and atheism, the apostasy of these times. On 25 August 1997 Blessed Mary said:

God gives me this time as a gift to you, so that I may instruct and lead you on the path of salvation.

Prior to crossing the river, the Lord told Joshua to tell the people to make themselves ready for the river crossing by sanctifying themselves:
And Joshua said to the people: "Be sanctified. For tomorrow the Lord will accomplish miracles among you."

Blessed Mary on 2 April 2010 asked us to be ready:

By your surrender and prayer ennoble your body and perfect your soul. Be ready, my children.

At apparition sites such as Medjugorje and Garabandal, Blessed Mary promises to leave a permanent sign at the place of her apparition, the place where she, the Ark of the New Covenant, stood as she held back the torrent of the river spewed from Satan and made a pathway for her children to cross the "river". The Israelites crossed the river into the Promised Land. Is this the time when we cross the river and enter into Heaven?

In the Book of Joshua, a permanent monument was made at the spot where the priests who were carrying the Ark of the Covenant stood in the river Jordan as the Ark and the priests formed a "bridge" that permitted the people to cross the river.

Mirjana says this about how the New Ark Blessed Mary with the help of the priests will form the "bridge" that permits us to cross over to Our Lady's final triumph:

> When we look at Our Lady's messages, when we talk about the privileged ones then we can talk about priests. Because Our Lady never said what they should do but only and always what we should do for them. ... they need you to pray for them and love them. My children, if you lose respect for priests, then you will lose respect for the church and in the end, Dear God as well.... Recently, almost every 2nd of the month, Our Lady has been emphasizing the importance of praying for priests.... she says do not forget to pray for your shepherds.... What I can say and you can make the same conclusion when you look at Our Lady's messages, between good and evil, between what is supposed to happen because you have to know what our Lady said, what she started in Fatima she will accomplish in Medjugorje. She said 'My Immaculate Heart will triumph'. So from this moment that we are now living until her triumph, there is a bridge and that bridge is the priests. And Our Lady decided we should pray for them so that this bridge may be firm, so that we can all cross that bridge to be able to reach, to come to Our Lady's triumph.

Our Lady will triumphantly lead her offspring into the promised land of heaven just as Esther triumphed over her adversary and delivered her people from annihilation. The priests will "carry" the Ark of the New

Covenant as a bridge across the river, which will be rolled back all the way to Adam at the time of the harvest. Our timeline stops at the end of the harvest of Sukkot. Is that when we cross the symbolic swollen river and enter into the Promised Land?

In conclusion, using typology and private revelation the passage from Revelation above could be worded this way:

And a great sign appeared in heaven: Blessed Mary at Fatima and at Medjugorje. And with the coming of the King of all nations imminent, the Church suffered tribulations of false prophets, great martyrdom, and apostasy. The people of God endured this trial in the wilderness that lasted for a time, times, and a half time throughout the twentieth century and beyond where many died, with the sustaining nourishment of the daily bread of the Holy Eucharist and the other sacraments. During this time of Satan, greed, terror, drugs, and modernism swept away the world. It tried to sweep away the Church too, but by simple faith the people of God persevered and they stood on the bank of the river swollen with the harvest rains, and were not swept away. With the support of the priests of the Church, Blessed Mary, the Ark of the New Covenant intercepted and blocked this river of filth spewed out of the evil one and kept it from sweeping us away—Our Lady triumphed over it. Through her intercession in the river (messages, the great warning, the great miracle) with her Son she restored things back to the original creation at the time of Adam. (Elijah will come to restore all things.) And in commemoration of this great event when with the aid of Blessed Mary, the New Covenant was fulfilled and the people of God crossed the river of evil, God left a permanent sign at the place of these apparitions.

Chapter 20
Musings on Garabandal

Garabandal, Spain, the site of an alleged apparition of Blessed Mary in the 1960s, has not been approved by the Catholic Church as worthy of belief, nor has it been ruled out as a supernatural occurrence. The Church's stance on Garabandal is neutral, so to speak. With that said, Garabandal could provide an answer to a problematic issue for those who speculate on the end times. The Jewish people, at least a large number of them, will recognize Jesus as the Messiah before the Last Day. The *Catechism of the Catholic Church* addresses this:

> The glorious Messiah's coming is suspended at every moment of history until his recognition by "all Israel", for "a hardening has come upon part of Israel" in their "unbelief" toward Jesus... The "full inclusion" of the Jews in the Messiah's salvation, in the wake of "the full number of the Gentiles", will enable the People of God to achieve "the measure of the stature of the fullness of Christ", in which "God may be all in all".[248]

After two-thousand years during which time the Jews faced many periods of persecutions and forced conversions to Christianity, they remain intractable on the issue of Jesus being the Messiah, leading most who study this issue to conclude it will take an act of God for the "full inclusion" of the Jews. This is where the apparition of Garabandal comes

---

[248] *Catechism* 674.

in for it was here for the first time in the long history of Marian apparitions, that Blessed Mary identified herself as Jewish, saying that even in heaven she belonged to the Jewish people.

From what the Garabandal visionaries said, there will be a warning, a miracle "marked" as it were by a great sign, and a chastisement, in that order. As for a time frame of when this might occur, Garabandal visionary Conchita Gonzalez-Keena is to announce the miracle eight days in advance, and as of this writing she is in her sixties. Notice that the visionaries at Medjugorje also say there will be warnings, a miracle "marked" by a great sign, and chastisements, in the same order. Seers from both apparitions are very likely describing the same events. As for the great sign that follows the miracle, they describe it as permanent, beautiful, and indestructible. The sign is expected to appear at several places of Marian apparitions, and all who see it will know it is from God rather than from the hands of man.

The Warning, Miracle and Sign

The warning has been described in this manner:

From the accounts of the Garabandal seers The Warning will be both a visible and interior experience for all of us in that we will see ourselves as God sees us and become aware of how we have sinned against a Most Loving and Generous God ... The Blessed Mother told visionary Conchita that The Warning will be a purification whereby we will see the consequences of our sins, that it is a "correction of the conscience of the world."

This experience will be supernatural ... This clearly miraculous origin will stamp The Warning as a divine admonition from God that we must amend our lives and turn from our sinful ways. We will feel remorse for those ways and want to become better people. Although a fearful external and internal experience, Our Blessed Mother made it clear to the seers that The Warning was a visible demonstration of God's generous mercy and compassion for His children ... [249]

---

[249] "The Warning: Our Upcoming Damascus." April 5, 2010.
<www.ourlady.ca/info/upcomingDamascus.htm>

And Garabandal visionary Mari-Loli said this about the warning, on 27 July 1975:

"Yes [I am afraid of the Warning]. Like everyone else I have faults, and the Warning will show me my faults and this makes me afraid...it is very important that we prepare ourselves because ... [it] will make us feel all the wrong we have done. [To prepare] one should do much penance, make sacrifices, visit the Blessed Sacrament every day that we are able to, and to pray the holy rosary daily... It will look as if the world has come to a standstill...no one will be aware of that as they will be totally absorbed in their own experience... God will help us to see clearly the harm we are causing Him and all the evil things we do. He will help us to sense this interior pain because often when we do something wrong we just ask the Lord's forgiveness with our lips, but through the Warning He will help us sense physically that deep sorrow."

In 1973 Conchita said, "The Warning will be...like a purification before the Miracle to see if with the Warning and Miracle we (meaning the whole world) will be converted."[250]

Not much is known about the miracle except that the sick present at the pines in Garabandal that day will be cured, and many unbelievers will be converted. All those either in the village or on the surrounding mountains will see the miracle. It will happen together with an ecclesiastical event in the Church akin to the declaration of a dogma, which will not happen as a consequence of the Miracle but only coincidentally. The purpose of the miracle is to convert the world.

The Timing of the Warning, Miracle and Sign

As for the timing of these events, over the years the Garabandal visionaries have revealed somewhat puzzling bits of information. The warning will occur less than a year before the miracle. And the miracle will occur on a Thursday evening at 8:30 on or between the eighth and the sixteenth of April on the feast day of a martyr of the Eucharist.[251]

---

[250] "The Warning and Miracle: Interviews with Seers." April 5, 2010.
<www.ourlady.ca/info/warning&miracle2.htm>
[251] Garabandal.org Information on the Apparitions of Garabandal -- St. Michael's Garabandal Center, November 12, 2010. <www.garabandal.org/miracle.shtml>

Because our timeline ends in 2017, looking at April 2017, the only Thursday between April 8 and April 16 falls on April 13. This date is interesting. Immediately one is reminded that the thirteenth of the month is heavily associated with the apparitions at Fatima. The next thing to note about 13 April 2017 is that it is Holy Thursday. Conchita said the miracle would be on the feast day of a martyr of the Eucharist. On Holy Thursday, Jesus instituted the Eucharist so He can be said to be the ultimate martyr of the Eucharist, since He is the Eucharist and He died on the cross the next day.

But Conchita ruled out Jesus when she revealed this about the Eucharistic martyr:

> The Miracle will be on the feast day of a young martyr of the Eucharist, a boy who carried Communion to persecuted Christians. His companions, on seeing him pass by, wanted to force him to stay and take part in their games. Infuriated by his resistance, they ended up hurling stones at him until he was left almost dead. Later a Christian soldier came, who recognized him and carried him in his arms.[252]

That best describes Saint Tarcisius. His feast day is celebrated on August 15, the feast day of the Assumption of Blessed Mary. However, the actual day of death for St. Tarcisius is a mystery. When the day of death is unknown for a martyr, the Church often selects another date. Because no one knows the day St. Tarcisius died the exact date of the miracle foretold in Garabandal cannot be known with any degree of certainty. It is quite possible that Tarcisius, forgotten by many because his feast day is "buried" by a solemn feast of Mary, will become better known on this day of the great miracle. In fact God might glorify him in a special way on that day when we celebrate the institution of the Eucharist, specifically because he gave up everything in defense of the Eucharist—namely, his young life.

We have noted the back-to-back Jewish feasts of Shemini Atzeret and Simchat Torah occur on 12 and 13 October 2017, and we are speculating that it is possible the Holy Spirit will descend upon the earth on that day. Simchat Torah is also known as the feast of the Last Great Day, and we have speculated that it is on this traditional Jewish feast day that the

---

[252] The Workers of Our Lady. Canada. "With the Miracle in Sight."
<www.ourlady.ca/info/book3/three07e-withMiracleSight.htm>

Triumph of the Immaculate Heart of Mary or more, such as the actual Last Day of this present world, might occur. Six months before that on 13 April 2017, a great miracle ("the greatest miracle ever done by Jesus in the world" according to one Garabandal seer) might very well occur, leading many to amend their lives and turn back to God.

The Day of Atonement

Speculatively, then, we are placing the miracle on Holy Thursday, 13 April 2017. The warning that precedes it can best be described as an affliction of our souls. Affliction means a state of pain, distress, or grief; misery; a cause of mental or bodily pain.[253] The warning takes place within one year of the miracle. Looking back one year in time over a calendar of religious feast days in search of a day matching that description, 12 October 2016 jumps out for two reasons. For one, it is exactly one year before Shemini Atzeret/Simchat Torah of October 12 and 13, 2017. Second, it is Yom Kipper, the Jewish Day of Atonement and the holiest and most solemn day of the year in all of Judaism (Remember, we are exploring the possibility that events foretold by the Garabandal apparition are the acts of God that lead to the "full inclusion" of the Jews before Jesus' return.) The warning entails an examination of our consciences before God to reveal our sins, so that we might improve. Yom Kippur is a day of honest self-examination, communication with one's Maker, and commitment to become a better person. It is a day exclusively emphasizing one's inner life. Similarly, the warning will be an interior occurrence. Yom Kippur is also among the most joyous days in Judaism as it affords one the opportunity to rectify past wrongs and face the future with a slate wiped clean.

Because the description of the warning matches to a large extent the meaning behind the feast of Yom Kippur and because it falls in the 2016/2017 time frame a year to the day before the Jewish Feast of the Last Great Day of 13 October 2017, it is not entirely unreasonable to conclude that the warning of Garabandal will occur on 12 October 2016.

As night falls at the end of each Yom Kippur, the age-old wish of Jews around the world, "Next year in the rebuilt Jerusalem," is proclaimed. When they say this on 12 October 2016, it might actually come to pass—the "new Jerusalem" just might come into existence one year later.

---

[253] Dictionary.com, April 5, 2010. <dictionary.reference.com/browse/affliction>

The Sign of the Son of Man and the Day of Atonement

The heart of Jesus was pierced for our transgressions on Good Friday and as we say in the "Litany of the Sacred Heart of Jesus" prayer: Heart of Jesus, atonement for our sins, have mercy on us.[254] The cross is the Christian sign of our atonement. In the 1930s, Jesus said to St. Faustina:

> Write this: before I come as the just Judge, I am coming first as the King of Mercy. Before the day of justice arrives, there will be given to people a sign in the heavens of this sort.

> All light in the heavens will be extinguished, and there will be great darkness over the whole earth. Then the sign of the cross will be seen in the sky, and from the openings where the hands and the feet of the Savior were nailed will come forth great lights which will light up the earth for a period of time. This will take place shortly before the last day. (Diary, #83) [255]

This coincides with Matthew 24 where Jesus, while speaking of the end times said that shortly before His coming on clouds in glory, "the sign of the Son of Man will appear in heaven."[256]

Visionary Jacinta from Garabandal (not to be confused with Jacinta of Fatima) said of the Garabandal warning:

> "The Warning is something that is first seen in the air everywhere in the world and immediately is transmitted into the interior of our souls."[257]

Compare this to what Jesus said—the sign of the cross, the sign of the Son of man, would be seen in the sky everywhere in the world. Of the heart of Jesus pierced on the cross, St Faustina writes:

> O Blood and Water, which gushed forth from the Heart of Jesus as a fount of mercy for us, I trust in You! (Diary, #84)[258]

---

[254] USCCB-(Liturgy)-Prayers Before the Blessed Sacrament, April 5, 2010. www.usccb.org/liturgy/prayerseucharist.shtml
[255] Kowalska, *Diary*, 83.
[256] USCCB-NAB-Matthew 24:30
[257] "Garabandal Apparition Prophecy: The Warning." June 17, 2010. <www.stjosephpublications.com/warning_page.htm>
[258] Kowalksa, *Diary*, 84.

From Sacred Scripture:

And I will pour out upon the house of David, and upon the inhabitants of Jerusalem, the spirit of grace, and of prayers: and they shall look upon me, whom they have pierced: and they shall mourn ... [259]
In that day there shall be a fountain open to the house of David, and to the inhabitants of Jerusalem: for the washing of the sinner. [260]

Washing of the sinner means atonement. The sign of the cross that will appear in the sky shortly before the last day as the sign of His Mercy is a sign of atonement, and so it would be fitting if the sign of the cross were to appear on the Jewish Day of Atonement.

What would be the impact on the Jewish people if the sign of the cross—the Christian sign of atonement—appeared in the sky on the Jewish Day of Atonement, followed at the same time with an interior examination of conscience with the Living God? Could this be the merciful act of God that will bring about the "full inclusion" of the Jews in the Messiah's salvation?

There is also a Day of Atonement on 30 September 2017 which is only thirteen days before 13 October, so it too is of intererst.

This is speculation (hence the word musings), and there is no way to know exactly what will happen.

The Pillar of Smoke and Our Lady of the Pillar

And I will work wonders in the heavens and on the earth, blood, fire, and columns of smoke; The sun will be turned to darkness, and the moon to blood, At the coming of the Day of the LORD, the great and terrible day. [261]

The Shekinah Glory is the sign of the tangible presence of the Glory of the living God. The Shekinah Glory, the "pillar of cloud by day and of fire by night," led Moses and the Hebrews out of Egypt and through the desert to Mount Sinai where they were given the Torah, and it stayed among them serving as their guide wherever they halted on their journey through the desert. It was the Lord who appeared to them in the pillar of cloud and

---

[259] Douay-Rheims Bible, Prophecy Of Zacharias Chapter 12:10, February 22, 2010. <www.drbo.org/chapter/43013.htm>
[260] Douay-Rheims Bible, Prophecy Of Zacharias Chapter 13:1
[261] USCCB-NAB-Joel 3:3-5, April 5, 2010. <www.usccb.org/nab/bible/joel/joel3.htm>

smoke. Jews throughout the world know the significance of the Shekinah Glory.

During the course of the alleged Garabandal apparitions in the early 1960s, several people saw what could only be described as a pillar of smoke above the pine trees at Garabandal during the day, and a pillar of fire over the area at night. Conchita revealed that although the sign can be compared to a "pillar of smoke" or to "rays of sunlight" it will not actually be either of these. This hints that it might in fact be the Shekinah Glory. It is entirely possible that the Shekinah Glory might appear at Garabandal on 13 April 2017 as the promised sign, and if so, this sign would help to convert the Jewish people. Fittingly, the Shekinah Glory led the Jews to the Promised Land—a type for heaven—and in a few years time it might reappear and this time lead the Jewish people to the Messiah, and then to the promised land of heaven itself.

The most significant religious feast day in Spain is Our Lady of the Pillar, celebrated on — October 12! According to an ancient local tradition, the Virgin appeared to James the Apostle in Zaragoza to console him, and she promised him her help and maternal assistance in his works of Apostolic preaching. Even more, as a signal of protection she left him a marble column that through the centuries has given the Shrine its name. Since then Our Lady of Pilar in Zaragoza, as it is commonly called in Spain, is considered the symbol of the firmness and constancy of the faith of the Spanish people and moreover it is an indication of the road that leads to the knowledge of Christ through the Apostolic teaching.[262]

What does the feast day of Our Lady of Pilar on 12 October have to do with a pillar of fire and smoke appearing on 13 April? On 7 February 1974 Conchita said: "For the words of the Blessed Mother to be complete, there must be the Warning and the Miracle. It is all one message."[263] The warning is the purification for the miracle—they are two parts of the same message. This means delivery of the message could start on Yom Kippur on 12 October 2016, the Spanish feast of Our Lady of the Pillar, and finish six months later on 13 April 2017 with the appearance of the "pillar of cloud by day and of fire by night", the Shekinah Glory.

John Paul II can be called Pope of the Pillar because he made four visits to the Shrine, two of which were personal. On his 6 November 1982

---

[262] Our Lady of Pilar, September 15, 2010. < www.apparitions-of-our-lady.com/our-lady-of-pilar.html>
[263] The Warning and Miracle - Interviews with Seers, November 12, 2010.
<www.ourlady.ca/info/warning&miracle2.htm>

pilgrimage to the holy Shrine of Our Lady of the Pillar, he touched upon its mystical nature when he said:

> The Spanish Christians have seen in the Pilar a clear analogy with the column that guided the people of Israel in their pilgrimage to the Promised Land. Therefore, through the centuries, they have been able to sing "Columnam disciples habemus," we have as a guide a Column that accompanies us to the new Israel.[264]

Conclusion

At Garabandal like in no other place Blessed Mary emphasized her Jewish nature, leading some to believe the apparition has special significance with regard to the "full inclusion" of the Jews in the Messiah's salvation. Our Lady of the Pillar is the world's first known apparition of Blessed Mary. Will her last apparition be the same as her first— in Spain, atop a pillar — this time the pillar of cloud by day and of fire by night— the Shekinah Glory— as she guides her children, and especially her Jewish kin, safely "home"?

Lucia died on 13 February 2005. That date on the Jewish calendar falls in the month of Adar. Could Lucia's death on the thirteenth day in the Gregorian calendar, during the Jewish month of Adar, serve as a signpost pointing to Esther and to that day's importance to both Gentile and Jew? Can there be hiding in plain sight another typological meaning in the Book of Esther? Christians and Jews often forget Blessed Mary's Jewish roots so in a sense her ethnicity is hidden, just as Esther's was hidden from the king (the name Esther means hidden.) Will Queen Mary, unheralded by those of her race, intercede to save her people the Jews, as well as her spiritual children the Christians? Is it through the intervention of Blessed Mary the New Ark that the Jews of our time will be led to Jesus the Messiah and be included in the Messiah's salvation?

Again, it was at Garabandal that Blessed Mary identified herself as Jewish, saying that even in heaven she belonged to the Jewish people.

---

[264] Ibid.

Chapter 21
Signs and Wonders

Joel mentions wonders in the heavens and on the earth, blood, fire, and columns of smoke as signs of the coming of the Day of the Lord, the Last Great Day. In the twentieth century, at the Marian apparition sites of Fatima, Garabandal, and Medjugorje, signs and wonders have been reported. The following is a small sampling of what has been reported at apparition sites.

While Fatima's great miracle of the sun, witnessed by 70,000 people, continues to be the greatest "sign and wonder" since the Apostles walked the earth, there have been others signs too.

At Fatima:

> It amazes me why this essential aspect hasn't been examined and proved. I refer to the manifestation of the pillar of smoke, like incense, at the place in Fatima, moments before the apparitions of the Virgin to the children. It has happened at all six of the apparitions on the days and times foretold.[265]

And also:

---

[265] Martins, Documents on Fatima & the Memoirs of Sister Lucia, 230.All rights reserved. Used with permission.

It must have been half past one when a column of smoke rose precisely from the spot where the children were. It was a thin, feeble, bluish column that rose straight up, two meters perhaps, above the heads of the people, and then broke up.

This phenomenon, clearly visible to the naked eye, lasted a few seconds ... The smoke broke up quickly and after a while the phenomenon repeated itself a second time and a third time.

I trained my binoculars on the spot. I saw nothing except the columns of smoke. I was convinced that they were produced by some motionless thurible in which incense was being burned.

Later on, trustworthy people assured me that it was usual for the thing to happen on the thirteenth of the five previous months, and that on those days, as on this one, nothing had ever been burned there nor had there ever been even a fire.[266]

At Garabandal, a sampling of some phenomena:

The account of what Mother Maria Nieves Garcia experienced on her visit to Garabandal in 1967. Here is her testimony.

At 2:00 p.m., on August 2, 1967, I was in a group of people walking up the hill from Cosio to Garabandal on a very sunny day. There wasn't a cloud in the sky, and I was feeling close to sunstroke. Just before we arrived at Garabandal, I looked at the sky and saw what everyone else in our group saw — a double rainbow around the sun. We could look at it without any eyestrain ... We were all able to observe the phenomenon without any strain on our eyes. I warned them, 'Be careful not to damage your eyes!' and they responded 'It's not hurting us at all.' Is this possible? A double rainbow around the sun at the beginning of August, without any clouds, at two in the afternoon? How curious that we all could look at it without any difficulty.[267]

And from Garabandal visionary Conchita's diary:

---

[266] Ibid, 214–215
[267] "A Special Place." April 5, 2010. <www.ourlady.ca/info/Special%20Place%20Jan09.htm>

During one of our apparitions, as Loli and I were coming down from the pines with a large number of people, we saw a thing like fire in the clouds. The people who were with us saw it, and so did those who weren't with us. [The Virgin] told us that is what she came in.

From Medjugorje:

When I visited the village in 1989 I was startled the first night to_see the full moon split and form two orbs. Fearing I was encountering an illusion, the result of jetlag, I called to another pilgrim and asked what she saw. The woman witnessed the same thing without my telling her what I was seeing. In the orb to the left was what both of us swore was the profile of a veiled woman. We both knew who that symbolized, but in the right I saw the profile of what looked like a bearded man...the next day visiting a church in nearby Tihaljina, I encountered two large statues in front of the altar, one of the veiled Virgin to the left, and at the other side, as in the other orb, a statue of a bearded man who I learned was the prophet Elijah.[268]

It is significant that Michael Brown saw Blessed Mary as an antitype of Elijah. Her role at this time is that of Elijah as described in Malachi, that of the messenger heralding the arrival of the Messiah. In the vision Elijah and Blessed Mary emanated from the one moon because Blessed Mary typologically is the Elijah who will come and restore all things.

Fire was seen in the sky at Medjugorje:

On August 6, 1981, the word MIR (peace) was written in the sky and seen by many people. It was on this day, during the apparition to the visionaries that Our Lady gave Her title for the first time, saying: "I am the Queen of Peace." Father Jozo stated:

"I remember when we saw the word MIR (peace) written in big, burning letters in the sky over the Cross on Mt. Krizevac. We were shocked. The moments passed, but we were unable to speak. No one dared say a word. Slowly, we came to our senses. We realized that we were still alive."

---

[268] Michael H. Brown, *The Final Hour*. (Milford, OH: Faith Publishing Company, 1992), 251–252.

In addition, although from descriptions it does not seem as extraordinary as that which occurred at Fatima, many thousands in Medjugorje have reported seeing the sun "dance" and "spin."

This is but a small sampling of the signs and wonders associated with these events. Many more have been reported, too many to cover in detail here.

Chapter 22
Fatima—In Conclusion

One finds the meaning of Fatima in eschatology. From Fatima comes the greatest miracle since the time of the Apostles. But why?

Fatima:

- reveals that Elijah is here, the Elijah who will restore all things
- reveals Blessed Mary is the typological Elijah who is to come
- reveals the meaning of the time, times and a half time by the dates of its key events
- reveals how the great tribulation gets cut short
- explains these times (tribulation, war, famine, church persecutions, persecutions of the Holy Father) as the Short Time of Satan of Revelation 20
- sets a boundary for these events. By relating it to Saint Margaret Mary's 100 years to the day, indicates its arc spans 100 years, to the date of the Miracle of the Sun. This ties in with Jesus saying one generation will see all these things; nation against nation, tribulation that is cut short, apostasy, the sign of the Son of Man. Biblically, a generation can be defined as being from the time of birth until the time of birth of the first child. Abraham fathered a son in his one-hundredth year. In the Olivet Discourse, Jesus was referring to both the generation of His day, and to the "generation"—the hundred years—of the time of the end.

- previews the Last Day—some are saved, some are not (those who feared the sun of 13 October 1917 are those who would have been lost; those who did not fear, saved)
- previews the Triumph of Mary—the Miracle of the Sun, the sun of justice with its healing rays
- along with its fulfillment through the period of peace, the apparitions of Medjugorje, it reveals the Woman of Revelation 12
- reveals the sun of justice: the apparitions of Fatima and Medjugorje often show the dancing sun, to remind us of the sun of justice of Malachi, and the fire of the end. This serves to underscore where we are on the end times arc—that the sun of justice of Malachi is about to come upon us, so be ready, be purified while there is still a little time.

In 2010, Pope Benedict XVI said Fatima is not over. Looking back at the events of the twentieth century it becomes more and more clear that Fatima is the singular event of the century, and post-Apostolic salvation history. The atrocities were so numerous they became commonplace, the norm rather than the exception. The century was the most horrific in the annals of man, surely a century of Satan. Now we await the conclusion of these events: the Triumph of the Immaculate Heart of Mary.

Chapter 23
The Third Temple

Since the destruction of the Second Temple, devout Jews and some branches of Christianity have desired to see a Third Temple built on the Temple Mount. But the Third Temple is here. The building of the Third Temple has made steady progress over the two thousand years of the Church Age. Christ and the mystical Body of Christ (the people of the Church) form the New Temple.

God's plan of salvation history is revealed in the Old and New Testaments. The New Covenant fulfills the promise given in the Old. This is seen by the typological use of key elements in the story of the Old Testament. In the New Testament we see the perfected manifestation of these elements as they take on flesh and blood. *[Our God] is not a God of the dead, but of the living, for to him all are alive.*[269]

A comparison of the key elements in both Testaments:

Old: Torah, the written word of God given to the Israelites

New: Jesus, the Word of God *...the Word was God. He was in the beginning with God*[270].

Old: Ark of the Covenant, with the indwelling of God

New: Mary, the Ark of the New Covenant, in whom God dwells

---

[269] USCCB-NAB-Luke 20:38, April 10, 2011. <www.usccb.org/nab/bible/luke/luke20.htm>
[270] John 1:1-2

Old: Manna, daily bread given to the Israelites as they journeyed across the desert
New: Eucharist, which is Jesus, the living bread come down from heaven

Old: Commandments written by God in stone at Shavuot
New: Commandments written by God on our hearts at Pentecost (Shavuot)

Old: Temple
New: Ourselves, our bodies

Our bodies are the temples of God.

Do you not know that your body is a temple of the holy Spirit within you[271]

The Shekinah Glory rested first on the Ark of the Covenant as a manifestation of the indwelling of God in the Ark. Later when the Ark was moved to the Temple, the Shekinah Glory rested on the Temple, again to show the indwelling of God. At Pentecost, the Holy Spirit descended upon the disciples and entered each of them. They became the temples of the Holy Spirit, Who manifested Himself with a visible tongue of fire, the Shekinah Glory, which came to rest upon each of their heads.

The Ark was kept in the Temple, so the Temple housed a pot with manna, the commandments of God written on stone tablets, and Aaron's budded staff. The Temple was destroyed and we have become the new Temple. The living manna come down from Heaven is within us when we receive the Eucharist. The commandments of God have been written on our hearts. Lastly, Jesus has made us a Kingdom of priests.[272] Jesus is our High Priest, and His ministerial priests serve both Him and us, and the rest of us form the "common" priesthood. Our baptism commits us to making sacrifice to God through participation in the Eucharist and the other sacraments, and living a holy life of self-denial and active charity.

The temple that will be rebuilt prior to the return of Jesus alludes to the Kingdom of God, the mystical Body of Christ that will stretch across the globe at the time of His return. As for the anti-Christ residing in the Temple, I do not profess to know whether this refers to the great apostasy

---

[271] I Corinthians 6:19
[272] cf. Revelation 1:6

of believers (the rebuilt third Temple) or to an actual demonic possession, of some kind, of a believer. It seems likely that Scripture alludes to one of these two possibilities.

The final typology of the Second Temple is found in its burning in 70 CE. As the Second Temple was consumed by fire at the fulfillment of the Old Covenant, so too will the temple—Christ's mystical body—be consumed in fire that either perfects or destroys each of us at the fulfillment of the New Covenant, a fire that will usher in the descent of the New Jerusalem and the actual Temple of God, the Church Triumphant, which will come down from heaven.

As for the Ark of the Covenant turning up in the last days, that is most likely referring to its antitype, the Ark of the New Covenant, Blessed Mary. This has already been fulfilled—Our Lady is her with us now to help us through these trying times of Satan.

Chapter 24
Speculation

Nobody knows the future, but we can speculate. Here I offer some thoughts and speculation.

For a potential timeline of events to come we have 12 October 2016, Yom Kippur, possibly coinciding with the day of the warning of Garabandal. On this day as part of the warning, we might see the sign of the cross mentioned by Saint Faustina appear in the sky as the sign of atonement. This could also be one of the ten secrets given by Blessed Mary at Medjugorje, perhaps even the first secret. At Garabandal, seer Conchita said that when we see the Warning we'll know we have opened up the end of time. At Medjugorje, Mary said that when the secrets unfold Satan's reign in the world will be broken. At Garabandal, Conchita reported Jesus said the Miracle would convert the world. (This is most likely an example of hyperbolic speech similar to Romans "All have sinned" — while the majority of people have committed sin not all have, such as small children not yet at the age of reason. Jesus and Blessed Mary are other examples.)

Six months after the warning, on 13 April 2017, the miracle of Garabandal might occur. Speculatively, this could correspond to the third secret of Medjugorje which is predicted to be a great sign that will be permanent, indestructible, and visible. All who look upon it will know it is from God. It is said that healings will accompany the Medjugorje sign and the Garabandal sign and miracle.

There are many secrets of Medjugorje and after the miracle or great sign, these will begin to unfold. Jesus said He would come quickly, so once the events of the last days begin one would expect them to happen in rapid succession. One could surmise the chastisement mentioned at Garabandal corresponds to one of these secrets, or perhaps to the Last Great Day and its fiery descent of the Holy Spirit. In any case 13 October 2017, the Jewish Last Great Day which occurs 100 years to the day from the fiery descent of the sun at Fatima might correspond to the tenth secret of Medjugorje, said to be fixed and unchangeable.

* * *

The messages from God through Blessed Mary at Medjugorje are given once a month for the nations of the world. The Book of Revelation contains an interesting passage:

> *Then the angel showed me the river of life-giving water, sparkling like crystal, flowing from the throne of God and of the Lamb down the middle of its street. On either side of the river grew the tree of life that produces fruit twelve times a year, once each month; the leaves of the trees serve as medicine for the nations.*[273]

Does this refer to the monthly messages we are being given now as a kind of medicine to heal us? After all, the monthly messages persuade many to amend their lives and return to God.

* * *

The messages of Blessed Mary at Medjugorje might end on or about 25 March 2014, and the catastrophic secrets meant for the world could begin to unfold at that time. A few weeks later, on 15 April 2014, a total lunar eclipse occurs. A total lunar eclipse is known as a blood moon.

The date 15 April 2014 is half way — 3.5 years — between the seven years from 13 October 2010 to 13 October 2017. Are these seven years the final week of years, the seventieth week of Daniel, before the arrival of the Messiah? The date of the total lunar eclipse is also the first day of Passover, the day of the Passion of Our Lord. Will this blood moon mark the beginning of the Passion of His Church, the mystical Body of Christ, as the catastrophic secrets of Medjugorje begin to unfold? Does the blood moon

---

[273] USCCB-NAB-Revelation 22:1-2, May 8, 2010.
<www.usccb.org/nab/bible/revelation/revelation22.htm>

that comes precisely at the halfway point of the seven years mark the time when the mystical Body of Christ is "cut off" as in the Daniel "weeks" prophecy? Note that when Jesus died on the cross a blood moon rose over Jerusalem.

Also note 13 October 2011 falls on Sukkot I, the first day of the seven-day harvest feast of the Ingathering. Does this allude to the start of the seventieth week of years of Daniel?

Note the halo of the sun at noon at Fatima on 13 May 2011, the anniversary of the first apparition of Blessed Mary there in 1917. Does this also mark the start of seven years before the promised triumph of the Immaculate Heart of Mary?

Note too the spectacularly large fiery eruption on the surface of the sun on 7 June 2011, the forty-ninth and final day of the Jewish Counting of the Omer — the counting of the days to Pentecost. Pentecost is the next day, the fiftieth day. Does this allude to a future fiery decent of the Holy Spirit in a new Pentecost?

Are these some of the signs in the sun, the moon, and the stars that Jesus said would herald His return?

* * *

It is interesting that on 25 March 2016, the Feast of the Annunciation, the Crucifixion (Good Friday), and Shushan Purim (commemorating the deliverance of the Jews of Jerusalem and other walled cities from annihilation because of Queen Esther's intercession) all occur.

* * *

The trapped Chilean miners requested a statue of Blessed Mary and rosary beads, and the Pope personally sent them each a Rosary. At Fatima, Mary appeared under the title Our Lady of the Rosary. On the seventieth day, 13 October 2010, the anniversary of the Miracle of the Sun at Fatima, all thirty-three trapped miners emerged unharmed. According to some interpretations of the Book of Daniel, in the seventieth week the Messiah comes. Again, thirty-three is the "time" sub-period of time, times, and a half time, and it is the sub-period we are in now according to our timeline. Thirty-three is also the number in Leviticus associated with purification.

Seventy days after the rescue of 13 October 2010, a total lunar eclipse (blood moon) appeared on 21 December, the winter solstice and the darkest day (the longest night). The eclipse started at thirty-three minutes past the hour.

* * *

The Blessed Mother started giving messages to her children in March 1984. Blessed Mary spent thirty years as mother to Jesus before He began His public ministry. This could be a type for what is happening now, as Mary is now spending thirty years mothering the Mystical Body of Christ. I suspect there will be at least thirty years of messages for her children and then she will stop appearing and the secrets will begin to unfold. Thirty years from 25 March 1984 takes us to 25 March 2014. Three and a half years later, which is a length of time that approximates Jesus' public ministry, it is 13 October 2017. This would mean the thirty years Blessed Mary mothered Christ in her home were a type for the thirty years she mothered the mystical body of Christ (*Dear Children...*).

* * *

The Bible tells us that the stars are the handiwork of God and they bear His messages:

The heavens declare the glory of God; the sky proclaims its builder's craft. One day to the next conveys that message; one night to the next imparts that knowledge. There is no word or sound; no voice is heard; Yet their report goes forth through all the earth, their message, to the ends of the world.[274]

The star of Bethlehem is the most famous example of this. During the week of Sukkot (the Festival of Ingathering, associated with the harvest) in October 2017, Venus and Mars are in conjunction. Venus is often associated with Blessed Mary, and Mars with Satan. Does this foretell the Triumph of the Immaculate Heart of Mary over Satan around 13 October 2017, the hundredth anniversary of the Miracle of the Sun at Fatima? Again, Jesus said there would be signs in the sun and the moon and the stars that announce His return. This is not astrology. The Bible tells us in the passage above that God can use the celestial bodies that He created to speak His messages to us, should He so choose. God sometimes uses them

---

[274] USCCB-NAB-Psalm 19:2-5, April 27, 2010. <www.usccb.org/nab/bible/psalms/psalm19.htm>

to reveal His plans. Astrology is a perversion of this; it says we can use the stars to tell about ourselves. It is another case of man trying to be God.

Mars is associated with the Babylonian god Nergal, the evil god of destruction, war, and death. The Babylonians marked the night of the thirteenth of each month as his holy day, and that explains why the thirteenth of the month of Adar was chosen as the date for the eradication of the Jews in the Persian Empire. Instead, this became the date of the triumph of the Jews due to Queen Esther's intervention, celebrated yearly by Jews as Purim. Interestingly, combining what Blessed Mary said at Fatima about Russia, and Medjugorje about the century of Satan, ones sees Russia as Satan's chosen instrument of persecution. Nergal carries a club, often depicted as a mallet-type of weapon, and sickle; the flag of Russia as the Soviet Union: the sledge hammer and sickle.

* * *

It is quite possible that the messages to the world from God through Mary will end on or about 25 March 2014. Hopefully, the remaining three and a half years before 13 October 2017 are not a time of an antichrist personage in imitation of the three and a half years of the public ministry of Jesus. I suspect at the least that they will be a time of great chaos, because it is likely the time when the catastrophic secrets of Medjugorje unfold. Note that this could be a period of time, times, and a half time lasting three and a half years nested within the larger time, times, and a half time that spans the twentieth century and runs until 13 October 2017—another example of the patterns of history repeating.

* * *

Thirty-three years after God consecrated the world through the annunciation to Blessed Mary, Jesus left the tomb in glory. Thirty-three years after the consecration of the world to the Immaculate Heart of Mary on the Feast of the Annunciation on 25 March 1984, does Jesus in some way come in glory, on 13 October 2017?

* * *

By considering Blessed Mary's use of the typology of Esther together with 13 October 2017 being the last yearly feast, Simchat Torah, can we merge the two and say the Triumph of Mary will be on the last day? "In the end my Immaculate Heart will triumph."

* * *

At the time of the Warning of Garabandal, which might also be when the secrets of Medjugorje unfold, we will know that we have "opened up the end of time," as seer Conchita of Garabandal said. But there is something more. Many think that Garabandal hints that a new Marian dogma will be proclaimed during the times of the warning and/or miracle associated with that apparition.

Since the 1920s to the present, more than 800 cardinals and bishops have petitioned various Popes for a new dogma, for an infallible definition of Mary's special maternal role in the salvation of humanity. In addition, the promoters of this devotion have gathered more than seven million petitions from faithful throughout the world.[275]

The movement for a fifth Marian dogma is a century old and it seems to be heading towards its culmination at the time of this writing. On 25 March 2010, the Vatican Forum of "Inside the Vatican" magazine and St. Thomas More College, in a meeting room close to St. Peter's Square, [invited] an international group of bishops and theologians to discuss whether now is the appropriate time for a fifth solemn definition or "dogma" to be pronounced regarding the Virgin Mary.[276]

Many proposing the dogma believe it will enable Blessed Mary to help her offspring during this time of apostasy. They believe that for Blessed Mary to intercede in a dramatic way without this dogma would be the same as God imposing Himself into our lives in a way that contradicts free will. On the other hand if the dogma is proclaimed, it is tantamount to us freely asking for God's intervention, at which point she will be empowered to provide it.

I suggest those who want to know more about this google it, or visit http://www.motherofallpeoples.com for more information. The timing of this is very interesting: if the fifth Marian dogma were proclaimed in the time before 13 October 2017, it might very well bring into being the

---

[275] "ZENIT - Is the Time Ripe for a 5th Marian Dogma?", November 18, 2010. <www.zenit.org/article-28508?l=english>
[276] Ibid.

Triumph of the Immaculate Heart of Mary over the world, resulting in a massive amount of conversions of souls.

* * *

About that number 13, interestingly there are 13 days between Yom Kippur and Simchat Torah. And in 2017 Hanukah, the Feast of Lights associated with the dedication of the Temple, occurs on December 13. Shushan Purim, associated with Esther, occurs on March 13. And as already discussed, April 13 is Holy Thursday.

* * *

There is something else I find intriguing. In the early days of the Medjugorje apparitions, visionary Mirjana asked for a sign. When her apparition ended, she noticed her watch had run backwards. This could be an indication of how time, times, and a half time flows in reverse.

But it also seems as if the glorious mysteries of the holy rosary are running backwards, too. Those mysteries are:
1. Resurrection of Jesus
2. Ascension of Jesus into Heaven
3. Descent of the Holy Spirit; tongues of fire appear over the disciples
4. Assumption of Blessed Mary's body and soul into Heaven
5. Coronation of Blessed Mary (crowned Queen of the Cosmos).

At Medjugorje, Blessed Mary is allegedly wearing a crown composed of twelve stars. She has returned bodily from heaven (the visionaries have said they can touch her, hold her hand, etc). The Assumption-in-reverse might be followed by the descent of the Holy Spirit upon the people of God, and then the descent or return of Jesus, followed by the resurrection of the mystical Body of Christ.

* * *

Another interesting thing to note is that Blessed Mary is allegedly appearing in Medjugorje, which is just ninety miles from Sarajevo. It was in Sarajevo that World War I ignited with the assassination of the archduke of Austria-Hungary, Franz Ferdinand, and his wife, Sophia, in 1914. In revelations to Berthe Pitt on 12 July 1912, Jesus purportedly spoke about it to her.

On that day, Jesus told Berthe that the heir to the Catholic empire of Austria-Hungary would be assassinated: *"A double murder will strike down the successor of the aged sovereign, so loyal to the faith."* He was referring to Archduke Franz Josef I (1830-1916), who was 82 years old at the time. Jesus added: *"It will be the first of those events full of sorrows, but from whence I shall still bring forth good and which will precede the chastisement."*[277]

This prophecy was fulfilled a little less than two years later on 28 June 1914 when a Serbian nationalist assassinated Archduke Franz Ferdinand and his wife Sophia. The following day Jesus said to Berthe, *"Now begins the ascending curve of preliminary events, which will lead to the great manifestation of My justice."*[278]

Could the phrase "great manifestation of My justice" refer to the Day of Judgment? In 1914 the archduke was assassinated, precipitating the rise of nation against nation. One hundred years from then, in 2014, Blessed Mary might stop appearing and the secrets of Medjugorje might begin to unfold, completing the ascending curve mentioned here by Jesus.

* * *

Again, a cautionary note: all of this is speculation on the part of the author. We do not, nor cannot, know dates and exact timings of future events; that is a realm reserved unto God. We can know with certainly that Blessed Mary promised her triumph, so it will come. We can know that one day Jesus will return for His bride, because He told us He would. And we can know that if we remain faithful to our Groom, we will be with Him in paradise, with all the saints.

---

[277] "The Sorrowful and Immaculate Heart of Mary: The Revelations of Berthe Petit." Sept. 22, 2010. <www.motherofallpeoples.com/index2.php?option=com_content&do_pdf=1&id=394>
[278] Ibid.

Chapter 25
Climb the Mountain!

Dear children! In the great love of God, I come to you today to lead you on the way of humility and meekness. The first station on that way, my children, is confession. Reject your arrogance and kneel down before my Son. Comprehend, my children, that you have nothing and you can do nothing. The only thing that is yours and what you possess is sin. Be cleansed and accept meekness and humility. My Son could have won with strength, but He chose meekness, humility and love. Follow my Son and give me your hands so that, together, we may climb the mountain and win! Thank you. (Blessed Mary, 2 July 2007)

According to Mirjana, Our Lady was referring to the spiritual climb when she spoke of "*climbing the mountain.*" Through the visionaries, Our Lady has stated that Medjugorje is the continuation of Fatima, and this has been particularly evident in the latest messages to Mirjana which seem to mirror the secret of Fatima.

The last part of the secret of Fatima contains the following image of climbing a mountain, in the words of Sister Lucia:

> *...Other Bishops, Priests, men and women Religious going up a steep mountain, at the top of which there was a big Cross... Beneath the two arms of the Cross there were two Angels each with a crystal aspersorium in his hand, in which they gathered up the blood of the Martyrs and with it sprinkled the souls that were making their way to God.*

This part of the secret is connected to the message of 2 July 2007, and it provides a description of Cross Mountain, which towers over Medjugorje. The countless pilgrims who make their way to Medjugorje often view climbing Cross Mountain as a means of reconciliation and penance.

The scene of the creation of the Old Covenant filled the people of Israel with great fear. Encamped at the foot of Mount Sinai, amidst deafening thunder and bright lightning flashes, they watched as a dark cloud descended upon the mountain, and from within the cloud came the sound of trumpets. The people trembled.

The smoke cloud ascended into the air, and the entire mountain shook violently. The trumpets became deafening, and then the Lord's voice spoke to Moses, sounding like thunder. At God's instructions, the mountain was declared consecrated to the Lord and a boundary was placed around the mountain as a warning not to touch it. It was upon this mountain that God gave His people Israel the Torah. Moses read the Torah to the people, and they agreed to it. Then Moses sprinkled blood from sacrificial animals, the blood of the covenant, onto the altar of the Lord and onto the people.

The Book of Hebrews describes the terrifying scene the Israelites faced as they assembled at the foot of Mount Sinai, a mountain they could not touch:

> *You have not approached that which could not be touched and a blazing fire and gloomy darkness and storm and a trumpet blast and a voice speaking words such that those who heard begged that no message be further addressed to them, for they could not bear to hear the command: "If even an animal touches the mountain, it shall be stoned." Indeed, so fearful was the spectacle that Moses said, "I am terrified and trembling."*[279]

Hebrews goes on to exhort us to not be afraid because we have not approached that which could not be touched—Sinai of the Old Covenant —but that which can be touched—Mount Zion, the Kingdom of God of the New Covenant.

Moses sprinkled blood of the old covenant on the people, but the sprinkled blood in the Fatima vision is the blood of the new covenant "that speaks more eloquently than that of Abel." By this blood, if we do not reject it, we not only can approach but we are invited to climb the

---

[279] USCCB-NAB-Hebrews 12:18-21, February 21, 2011.
<www.usccb.org/nab/bible/hebrews/hebrews12.htm>

mountain and enter into the celestial kingdom at the top, the city of the living God!

No, you have approached Mount Zion and the city of the living God, the heavenly Jerusalem, and countless angels in festal gathering, and the assembly of the firstborn enrolled in heaven, and God the judge of all, and the spirits of the just made perfect, and Jesus, the mediator of a new covenant, and the sprinkled blood that speaks more eloquently than that of Abel.

See that you do not reject the one who speaks. For if they did not escape when they refused the one who warned them on earth, how much more in our case if we turn away from the one who warns from heaven.

His voice shook the earth at that time, but now he has promised, "I will once more shake not only earth but heaven." That phrase, "once more," points to (the) removal of shaken, created things, so that what is unshaken may remain. Therefore, we who are receiving the unshakable kingdom should have gratitude, with which we should offer worship pleasing to God in reverence and awe.
For our God is a consuming fire.[280]

This last verse takes us once more to the fiery descent of the sun at Fatima.

As a final appeal for adherence to Christian teaching, Hebrews compares the two covenants, of Moses and of Christ. The Mosaic covenant is shown to have originated in fear of God and threats of divine punishment.

But the covenant in Christ gives us direct access to God, makes us members of His kingdom, God's children, a sanctified people, who have Jesus as mediator to speak for us. It is a covenant that originates in love and mercy, the mercy of Jesus shown to us by His cross. Not to heed the loving voice of the merciful risen Christ is a graver sin than the rejection of the word of Moses. Though Christians fall away, God's kingdom in Christ will remain and his justice will punish with fire those guilty of rejecting His all-encompassing mercy. God gave us His only Son to save us, not to condemn us. We are free to reject His gift of mercy, but we do so at our peril.

The remarkably beautiful passage in Hebrews contrasts two great assemblies of people: that of the Israelites gathered at Mount Sinai for the

---

[280] Hebrews 12:22-29

sealing of the Old Covenant and the promulgation of the Mosaic law, and that of the followers of Jesus gathered at Mount Zion, the heavenly Jerusalem, the assembly of the New Covenant. This latter scene, marked by the presence of countless angels and of Jesus with his redeeming blood, is reminiscent of the celestial liturgies of the Book of Revelation.[281]

In a covenant, the one who breaks it deserves death. We people have broken our covenant with God and deserve death, but God said no, you have broken our covenant but I will die for you instead, because I love you so much. And God cannot die, but a death is required because the covenant has been broken. So God became man just so He could die for us, to restore our covenant with His blood, to restore the family of God. In the Old Covenant if the people or their animals so much as touched the mountain, they died. Now through Jesus Who by His death on the cross has become our mediator with the Father, we are invited to climb the mountain to God.

At Fatima Lucia saw the future, she saw us in our struggle to return to God in these times. God is inviting us to come to Him. Let us climb the mountain together with Blessed Mary and enter into that celestial Kingdom of Heaven at the top of the mountain, the city of the living God!

Dear children! In the great love of God, I come to you today to lead you on the way... follow my Son... give me your hands so that, together, we may climb the mountain and win!

Be Not Afraid!

---

[281] USCCB-NAB-Hebrews 12 Footnote 5, February 21, 2011.
<www.usccb.org/nab/bible/hebrews/hebrews12.htm#foot5>

PART III

Selected Messages from Medjugorje

There are literally thousands of messages from Blessed Mary over the last thirty years of apparitions. Here is but a select few. Resources with these messages abound—the internet, books, and videos. The website http://medjugorje.org/concordance/framconc.htm provides a concordance of the messages, allowing one to search for specific words.

Recent Messages

June 25, 2011, 30th anniversary: Dear children! Give thanks with me to the Most High for my presence with you. My heart is joyful watching the love and joy in the living of my messages. Many of you have responded, but I wait for, and seek, all the hearts that have fallen asleep to awaken from the sleep of unbelief. Little children, draw even closer to my Immaculate Heart so that I can lead all of you toward eternity. Thank you for having responded to my call.

May 25, 2011: Dear children! My prayer today is for all of you who seek the grace of conversion. You knock on the door of my heart, but without hope and prayer, in sin, and without the Sacrament of Reconciliation with God. Leave sin and decide, little children, for holiness. Only in this way can I help you, hear your prayers and seek intercession before the Most High. Thank you for having responded to my call.

May 02, 2011: Dear children; God the Father is sending me to show you the way of salvation, because He, my children, desires to save you and not to condemn you. That is why I, as a mother, am gathering you around me, because with my motherly love I desire to help you to be free of the dirtiness of the past and to begin to live anew and differently. I am calling you to resurrect in my Son. Along with confession of sins renounce everything that has distanced you from my Son and that has made your life empty and unsuccessful. Say 'yes' to the Father with the heart and set out on the way of salvation to which He is calling you through the Holy Spirit. Thank you. I am especially praying for the shepherds (priests), for God to help them to be alongside you with a fullness of heart.

February 02, 2011: Dear children; You are gathering around me, you are seeking your way, you are seeking, you are seeking the truth but are forgetting what is the most important, you are forgetting to pray properly. Your lips pronounce countless words, but your spirit does not feel anything. Wandering in darkness, you even imagine God Himself according to yourselves, and not such as He really is in His love. Dear children, proper prayer comes from the depth of your heart, from your suffering, from your joy, from your seeking the forgiveness of sins. This is the way to come to know the right God and by that also yourselves, because you are created according to Him. Prayer will bring you to the fulfillment of my desire, of my mission here with you, to the unity in God's family. Thank you.

[Our Lady blessed everyone present, thanked them and called us to pray for priests.]

March 02, 2011: Dear children; My motherly heart suffers tremendously as I look at my children who persistently put what is human before what is of God; at my children who, despite everything that surrounds them and despite all the signs that are sent to them, think that they can walk without my Son. They cannot! They are walking to eternal perdition. That is why I am gathering you, who are ready to open your heart to me, you who are ready to be apostles of my love, to help me; so that by living God's love you may be an example to those who do not know it. May fasting and prayer give you strength in that and I bless you with motherly blessing in the name of the Father and of the Son and of the Holy Spirit. Thank you.

[Our Lady was very sad.]

Messages on the Triumph of the Immaculate Heart of Mary

March 18, 2007: Dear children! I come to you as a Mother with gifts. I come with love and mercy. Dear children, mine is a big heart. In it, I desire all of your hearts, purified by fasting and prayer. I desire that, through love, our hearts may triumph together. I desire that through that triumph you may see the real Truth, the real Way and the real Life. I desire that you may see my Son. Thank you.

May 2, 2006: Dear children, I am coming to you as a mother. I am coming with an open heart full of love for you, my children. Cleanse your hearts from everything that prevents you from receiving me; from recognizing the love of my Son. Through you, my heart desires to win—desires to triumph. Open your hearts; I will lead you to this. Thank you!

Oct 2 2010: Dear Children, Today I call you to a humble, my children, humble devotion. Your hearts need to be just. May your crosses be your means in the battle against the sins of the present time. May your weapon be patience and boundless love—a love that knows to wait and which will make you capable of recognizing God's signs—that your life, by humble love, may show the truth to all those who seek it in the darkness of lies. My children, my apostles, help me to open the paths to my Son. Once again I call you to pray for your shepherds. Alongside them, I will triumph. Thank You.

June 2, 2007: Dear children! Also in this difficult time God's love sends me to you. My children, do not be afraid, I am with you. With complete trust give me your hearts, that I may help you to recognize the signs of the time in which you live. I will help you to come to know the love of my Son. I will triumph through you. Thank you.

[Our Lady blessed everyone present. Once again She reminded us to pray for priests and that a priest's blessing is a blessing from Her son, Jesus.]

April 2, 2007: Dear children, do not be of a hard heart towards the mercy of God, which has been pouring out upon you for so much of your time. In this special time of prayer, permit me to transform your hearts that you may help me to have my Son resurrect in all hearts, and that my heart may triumph. Thank you.

[Our Lady added: "Your Shepherds need your prayers".]

March 18, 2007: Dear children, I come to you as a Mother with gifts. I come with love and mercy. Dear children, mine is a big heart. In it, I desire all of your hearts, purified by fasting and prayer. I desire that, through love, our hearts may triumph together. I desire that through that triumph you may see the real Truth, the real Way and the real Life. I desire that you may see my Son. Thank you.

September 25, 2009: Dear children, with joy, persistently work on your conversion. Offer all your joys and sorrows to my Immaculate Heart that I may lead you all to my most beloved Son, so that you may find joy in His Heart. I am with you to instruct you and to lead you towards eternity. Thank you for having responded to my call.

Sin

October 2, 2009: Dear Children, As I look at you, my heart seizes with pain. Where are you going my children? Have you sunk so deeply into sin that you do not know how to stop yourselves? You justify yourselves with sin and live according to it. Kneel down beneath the Cross and look at my

Son. He conquered sin and died so that you, my children, may live. Permit me to help you not to die but to live with my Son forever. Thank you!

February 25, 1987: Dear children! Today I want to wrap you all in my mantle and lead you all along the way of conversion. Dear children, I beseech you, surrender to the Lord your entire past, all the evil that has accumulated in your hearts. I want each one of you to be happy, but in sin nobody can be happy. Therefore, dear children, pray, and in prayer you shall realize a new way of joy. Joy will manifest in your hearts and thus you shall be joyful witnesses of that which I and My Son want from each one of you. I am blessing you. Thank you for having responded to my call.

Return to the Father

November 2, 2009: Dear children, Also today I am among you to point you to the way that will help you to come to know God's love, the love of God Who permitted you to call Him Father and to perceive Him as Father. I ask of you to sincerely look into your hearts and to see how much you love Him. Is He the last to be loved? Surrounded by material goods, how many times have you betrayed, denied and forgotten Him? My children, do not deceive yourselves with worldly goods. Think of your soul because it is more important than the body, cleanse it. Invoke the Father, He is waiting for you. Come back to Him. I am with you because He, in His mercy, sends me. Thank you.

October 25, 1987: My dear children! Today I want to call all of you to decide for Paradise. The way is difficult for those who have not decided for God. Dear children, decide and believe that God is offering Himself to you in His fullness. You are invited and you need to answer the call of the Father, Who is calling you through me. Pray, because in prayer each one of you will be able to achieve complete love. I am blessing you and I desire to help you so that each one of you might be under my motherly mantle. Thank you for having responded to my call.

Messages Pertaining to Peace with God and Neighbor

June 25, 1987: Dear children! Today I thank you and I want to invite you all to God's peace. I want each one of you to experience in your heart that peace which God gives. I want to bless you all today. I am blessing you with God's blessing and I beseech you, dear children, to follow and to live my way. I love you, dear children, and so not even counting the number of times, I go on calling you and I thank you for all that you are doing for my intentions. I beg you, help me to present you to God and to save you. Thank you for having responded to my call.

April 25, 2009: Dear children! Today I call you all to pray for peace and to witness it in your families so that peace may become the highest treasure on this peaceless earth. I am your Queen of Peace and your mother. I desire to lead you on the way of peace, which comes only from God. Therefore, pray, pray, pray. Thank you for having responded to my call.

June 25, 2009: Dear children, I call you to be apostles of peace. Peace, peace, peace.

Sacrifice to Save Others

November 25, 1990: Dear children! Today I invite you to do works of mercy with love and out of love for me and for your and my brothers and sisters. Dear children, all that you do for others, do it with great joy and humility towards God. I am with you and day after day I offer your sacrifices and prayers to God for the salvation of the world. Thank you for having responded to my call.

February 25, 1988: Dear children! Today again I am calling you to prayer to complete surrender to God. You know that I love you and am coming here out of love so I could show you the path to peace and salvation for your souls. I want you to obey me and not permit Satan to seduce you. Dear children, Satan is very strong and, therefore, I ask you to dedicate your prayers to me so that those who are under his influence can be saved. Give witness by your life. Sacrifice your lives for the salvation of the world. I am with you, and I am grateful to you, but in heaven you shall receive the Father's reward which He has promised to you. Therefore, dear children, do not be afraid. If you pray, Satan
cannot injure you even a little bit because you are God's children and He is watching over you. Pray and let the rosary always be in your hand as a sign to Satan that you belong to me. Thank you for having responded to my call.

March 29, 1984: Dear children! In a special way this evening I am calling you to perseverance in trials. Consider how the Almighty is still suffering today on account of your sins. So when sufferings come, offer them up as a sacrifice to God. Thank you for having responded to my call.

June 25, 2005: Dear children! Today I thank you for every sacrifice that you have offered for my intentions. I call you, little children, to be my apostles of peace and love in your families and in the world. Pray that the Holy Spirit may enlighten and lead you on the way of holiness. I am with you and bless you all with my motherly blessing. Thank you for having responded to my call.

May 25, 1996: Dear children! Today I wish to thank you for all your prayers and sacrifices that you, during this month which is consecrated to me, have offered to me. Little children, I also wish that you all become active during this time that is through me connected to heaven in a special way. Pray in order to understand that you all, through your life and your example, ought to collaborate in the work of salvation. Little children, I wish that all people convert and see me and my son, Jesus, in you. I will intercede for you and help you to become the light. In helping the other, your soul will also find salvation. Thank you for having responded to my call.

November 25, 1993: Dear children! I invite you in this time like never before to prepare for the coming of Jesus. Let little Jesus reign in your hearts and only then when Jesus is your friend will you be happy. It will not be difficult for you either to pray or offer sacrifices or to witness Jesus' greatness in your life because He will give you strength and joy in this time. I am close to you by my intercession and prayer and I love and bless all of you. Thank you for having responded to my call.

November 25, 1991: Dear Children! This time also I am inviting you to prayer. Pray that you might be able to comprehend what God desires to tell you through my presence and through the messages I am giving you. I desire to draw you ever closer to Jesus and to His wounded heart that you might be able to comprehend the immeasurable love which gave itself for each one of you. Therefore, dear children, pray that from your heart would flow a fountain of love to every person both to the one who hates you and to the one who despises you. That way you will be able through Jesus' love to overcome all the misery in this world of sorrows, which is without hope for those who do not know Jesus. I am with you and I love you with the immeasurable love of Jesus. Thank you for all your sacrifices and prayers. Pray so I might be able to help you still more. Your prayers are necessary to me. Thank you for having responded to my call.

November 25, 1996: Dear children! Today, again, I invite you to pray, so that through prayer, fasting and small sacrifices you may prepare yourselves for the coming of Jesus. May this time, little children, be a time of grace for you. Use every moment and do good, for only in this way will you feel the birth of Jesus in your hearts. If with your life you give an example and become a sign of God's love, joy will prevail in the hearts of men. Thank you for having responded to my call.

Prayer

November 25, 1998 "Dear children! Today I call you to prepare yourselves for the coming of Jesus. In a special way, prepare your hearts. May holy Confession be the first act of conversion for you and then, dear children, decide for holiness. May your conversion and decision for holiness begin today and not tomorrow. Little children, I call you all to the way of salvation and I desire to show you the way to Heaven. That is why, little children, be mine and decide with me for holiness. Little children, accept prayer with seriousness and pray, pray, pray. Thank you for having responded to my call.

November 25, 2009: Dear children! In this time of grace I call you all to renew prayer in your families. Prepare yourselves with joy for the coming of Jesus. Little children, may your hearts be pure and pleasing, so that love and warmth may flow through you into every heart that is far from His love. Little children, be my extended hands, hands of love for all those who have become lost, who have no more faith and hope. Thank you for having responded to my call.

January 25, 2010: Dear children! May this time be a time of personal prayer for you, so that the seed of faith may grow in your hearts; and may it grow into a joyful witness to others. I am with you and I desire to inspire you all: grow and rejoice in the Lord Who has created you. Thank you for having responded to my call.

August 25, 2010: Dear children! With great joy, also today, I desire to call you anew: pray, pray, pray. May this time be a time of personal prayer for you. During the day, find a place where you will pray joyfully in a recollected way. I love you and bless you all. Thank you for having responded to my call.

July 25, 2009 Dear children! May this time be a time of prayer for you. Thank you for having responded to my call.

April 25, 1987: Dear children! Today also I am calling you to prayer. You know, dear children, that God grants special graces in prayer. Therefore, seek and pray in order that you may be able to comprehend all that I am giving here. I call you, dear children, to prayer with the heart. You know that without prayer you cannot comprehend all that God is planning through each one of you. Therefore, pray! I desire that through each one of you God's plan may be fulfilled, that all which God has planted in your heart may keep on growing. So pray that God's blessing may protect each one of you from all the evil that is threatening you. I bless you, dear children. Thank you for having responded to my call.

This Time

May 25, 2001: Dear children! At this time of grace, I call you to prayer. Little children, you work much but without God's blessing. Bless and seek the wisdom of the Holy Spirit to lead you at this time so that you may comprehend and live in the grace of this time. Convert, little children, and kneel in the silence of your hearts. Put God in the center of your being so that, in that way, you can witness in joy the beauty that God continually gives in your life. Thank you for having responded to my call.

June 25, 2001 "Dear children! I am with you and I bless you all with my motherly blessing. Especially today when God gives you abundant graces, pray and seek God through me. God gives you great graces, that is why, little children make good use of this time of grace and come closer to my heart so that I can lead you to my Son Jesus. Thank you for having responded to my call.

February 25, 2000: Dear children! Open your heart to God's mercy in this Lenten time. The heavenly Father desires to deliver each of you from the slavery of sin. Therefore, little children, make good use of this time and through meeting with God in confession, leave sin and decide for holiness. Do this out of love for Jesus, who redeemed you all with his blood, that you may be happy and in peace. Do not forget, little children: your freedom is your weakness, therefore follow my messages with seriousness. Thank you for having responded to my call.

June 25, 1992: Dear children! Today I am happy, even if in my heart there is still a little sadness for all those who have started on this path and then have left it. My presence here is to take you on a new path, the path to salvation. This is why I call you, day after day to conversion. But if you do not pray, you cannot say that you are on the way to being converted. I pray for you and I intercede to God for peace; first peace in your hearts and also peace around you, so that God may be your peace. Thank you for having responded to my call.

June 25, 1993: Dear children! Today I also rejoice at your presence here. I bless you with my motherly blessing and intercede for each one of you before God. I call you anew to live my messages and to put them into life and practice. I am with you and bless all of you day by day. Dear children, these are special times and, therefore, I am with you to love and protect you; to protect your hearts from Satan and to bring you all closer to the heart of my Son, Jesus. Thank you for having responded to my call.

Instruction

December 31, 1981: One cannot compel a person to believe. Faith is the foundation from which everything flows.

June 25,1991: Dear children! Today on this great day which you have given to me, I desire to bless all of you and to say: these days while I am with you are days of grace. I desire to teach you and help you to walk the way of holiness. There are many people who do not desire to understand my messages and to accept with seriousness what I am saying. But you I therefore call and ask that by your lives and by your daily living you witness my presence. If you pray, God will help you to discover the true reason for my coming. Therefore, little children, pray and read the Sacred Scriptures so that through my coming you discover the message in Sacred Scripture for you. Thank you for having responded to my call.

July 24, 1982:
We go to Heaven in full conscience: that which we have now. At the moment of death, we are conscious of the separation of the body and the soul. It is false to teach people that we are re-born many times and that we pass to different bodies. One is born only once. The body, drawn from the earth, decomposes after death. It never comes back to life again. Man receives a transfigured body.

Also on July 24, 1982:
Whoever has done very much evil during his life can go straight to Heaven if he confesses, is sorry for what he has done, and receives Communion at the end of his life.

On 18 March, 2008, Our Lady extended her hands towards us and with her hands extended in this way, she said:

Dear children, today I extend my hands towards you. Do not be afraid to accept them. They desire to give you love and peace and to help you in salvation. Therefore, my children, receive them. Fill my heart with joy and I will lead you towards holiness. The way on which I lead you is difficult and full of temptations and falls. I will be with you and my hands will hold you. Be persevering so that, at the end of the way, we can all together, in joy and love, hold the hands of my Son. Come with me; fear not! Thank you!

Epilogue

At Sinai, God made a covenant with His people, who became His bride. This was the first part of the Jewish wedding, erusin, the betrothal. And what of the second part, nisuin, the wedding feast? When Jesus came to dwell with His bride Israel, both He and John the Baptist said He is the Bridegroom. At the synagogue, Jesus read from Isaiah about the Messiah and the jubilee He would bring, and then Jesus said He fulfilled the passage. The wedding feast at Cana was the nisuin part of the wedding, for it was here that Jesus performed His first miracle when He changed the water into wine: *On the third day there was a wedding at Cana in Galilee. The mother of Jesus was there, and Jesus and his disciples had also been invited. And they ran out of wine...and the mother of Jesus said to him, 'They have no wine'...This was the first of Jesus' signs: it was at Cana in Galilee. He revealed his glory, and his disciples believed in him.*[282]

Running out of wine is a type for lack of faith, for the broken covenant, for it is wine that becomes the blood of the new Covenant. When the Son of Man comes will He find any faith? At the wedding, Blessed Mary interceded, asking her Son to help. This is a type for Mary's intercessory role when she asks her Son to help as her offspring fall away just before the end of the age. Blessed Mary's first intercession at Cana is a type for her last, greatest intercession, the fulfillment of her intercessory role in the triumph of Her Immaculate Heart. And Jesus' first miracle at Cana could be a type for His last, greatest miracle, performed at the time of the end. Garabandal seer Conchita reported Jesus said His miracle there would be His greatest miracle, and it would convert much of the world. Conchita said the incredulous will believe and sinners will be converted.

The Bride, the builders, rejected the Groom, the cornerstone, but out of love Jesus proposed a new covenant with both Israel and the Gentiles, the nations. He made the covenant international, worldwide, catholic. His Church throughout the world, the bride of Christ, eagerly awaits His return.

And there shall be signs in the sun, and in the moon, and in the stars; and upon the earth distress of nations...But when these things begin to come to pass, look up, and lift up your heads, because your redemption is at hand.[283]

---

[282] John 2:1-3,5,11, June 25, 2010. <http://www.catholic.org/bible/book.php?id=35>
[283] Douay-Rheims Bible, Luke 21:25,28.

For further reading:

Queen of the Cosmos by Janice T. Connell

The Final Harvest by Wayne Weible

Messages and Teachings of Mary at Medjugorje by Rene Laurentin and Rene Lejeune

The Visions of the Children by Janice T. Connell

The Final Hour by Michael H. Brown

Documents on Fatima and the Memoirs of Sister Lucia by Father Antonio Maria Martins, S.J. with Updates by Father Robert J. Fox

"Calls" From the Message of Fatima by Sister Lucia

The End of the Present World and the Mysteries of the Future Life by Father Charles Arminjon

Diary: Divine Mercy in My Soul by Sister Maria Faustina Kowalska

The Catechism of the Catholic Church

Website with Concordance of the Messages of Blessed Mary at Medjugorje:
http://medjugorje.org/concordance/framconc.htm

Made in the USA
Charleston, SC
16 May 2012